GATHERED
FOR POWER

Bill Barnes
Aug 75

GATHERED FOR POWER

by
Graham Pulkingham

Illustrations by Cathleen

HODDER AND STOUGHTON
LONDON   SYDNEY   AUCKLAND   TORONTO

This book is dedicated to
Grace Murray who prayed much

and
Bob Evans who worked hard.

Contents

Foreword

Houston was on my schedule for a visit I made to the United States in 1966. I had never heard of the Church of the Redeemer, but a friend introduced me to it while I was there. My short stay convinced me that this church had found something—it was then quite formative, but I had not seen it anywhere else. Almost exactly six years later I returned to see the dream come true: a church girded for action, ministering powerfully to the neighborhood. For several weeks I was able to share with many of its members and see the fascinating way God's plan had unfolded.

Graham Pulkingham shares in this book the story of how he first came to the church, his earliest endeavours that ended in almost total failure, his honest approach to a powerless ministry, his turning to God—first in rage, then in faith to receive the power of the Holy Spirit, and his hearing God speaking to him. But perhaps the key to the whole story is to be found in a strange contradiction. First, there was his strong sense of call to the parish, verging on megalomania even to the point of feeling uniquely chosen for the task of its renewal, and second his willingness to lose that identity completely in submission to a shared or group ministry. The contradiction lies in this, having felt called of God for both, he relinquished neither, and when he reduced the position of rector to nominal headship, his sense of being uniquely chosen was transferred to the group.

This is the story of how a strong personality was humbled by failure, strengthened by the Spirit, and humbled again to share his ministry with others in such a manner that it was no longer his. From that, a body of servants was "gathered for power."

Although this is an intensely human story, God's grace is the only obvious explanation for what happened. That such a person should succeed in a parish which by all commonly accepted standards today was doomed to failure and extinction, is a miracle of the highest order. One can only conclude that God did it simply by His presence and power. If that is so, then this story should be studied carefully, for there are undoubtedly principles here which are applicable in many other situations.

This book, and the sequel that will follow it, has a message that it would be perilous indeed for the modern church to neglect.

Michael Harper

GATHERED
FOR POWER

Prelude

After I agreed to write the story of renewal in Houston's Redeemer Church, I gave some second thoughts to the matter and began to realize the intricacy of the task—either it is a single very ungainly story, or two or more shorter ones. Its complexity lies as much with things that are hidden as with such obvious considerations as abundance of material and fascinating detail. For example, the implications for the church at large—and the personal ramifications too—of the kind of life people have been living together in Redeemer fellowship for the past six years are enormous.

I am the rector of the parish, and am happy to report the last eight years of my life amount to mystery, of a kind I had not experienced before. By mystery I mean to say that to me it is plain that God has done the thing that has happened; and what has happened is plain to see. Certainly, my experience with Redeemer Church was not the first unusual thing that had ever happened to me and I know that God's grace has been at work in me throughout my life. But the changes brought about in these past few years are so dramatic that they are clear evidences of the presence and power of the Holy Spirit. I once heard the French master, Marcel Dupré perform an unprogrammed evening of great organ music.

Interspersed throughout the concert were several short compositions of his own. Before each work was begun the simple man stepped forward to announce the composer, date of composition, and title, but before his own pieces he said humbly, "Mine own." In the same spirit, hopefully, I would like to submit that the following events are, in the infinite and varied riches of the mystery of Christ, "Mine own."

Cardinal Suhard of the French worker-priest movement has said, "It is not the task of Christians to advocate a program or ideology. Rather their task is to create a mystery that cannot be explained by any human system of thinking and can finally only be understood as the grace of God."* True words and helpful, but I would ask Cardinal Suhard the question, "Understood by whom?" He must surely answer, "By Christians themselves, for only they can comprehend the grace of God." But is the mystery of His revealed will so limited? That is to say, is the Church's task simply to attest to the fact of grace? I think not, if I understand Paul's thinking in the third chapter of Ephesians. It seems to me that the explanation of the Christian's task since Pentecost lies not only with the fact of God's grace but also with the manifestation of His glory. The church must reveal mystery not only to itself, but to all men and to the unseen powers of the universe as well. A brief illustration of my point: I believe that when a person is healed through the ministration of a Christian Science practitioner, God's grace has been operative, but God has not been glorified—Christian Science has.

However, I see other less obvious possibilities for the usurpation of God's grace than Christian Science. There is a woman in America, called of God and given (I think to the Church, though she would probably disagree with me) to be an astonishing manifestation in our time of the healing gifts of the Holy Spirit. She is Kathryn Kuhlman, a unique and

*Quoted from Harvey Cox: *On Not Leaving It to the Snake*, p. 54

12

refreshing evangelist. Her fame is justifiable on the ground that the miracle associated with her ministry is plainly the result of her dedicated life and anointing by God. God is with her, and through a startling ministry associated with her name He receives the glory reserved only to Himself. That, I think, is at the heart of mystery. Only Kathryn Kuhlman can do what she does because only she has been called to do it— to the manifest glory of God the Father. Other people, for lack of a clearer vision, have begun to imitate her; though there may be amazing wonders attendant upon their words and actions, though their words and actions may be in every respect conformed to hers, I cannot associate their efforts with mystery because in their work the glory of God is hidden somewhere in the midst of exhibitionism and display. Though the glory is lost, grace is at work and God's mercy extends to granting works of faith even in situations like these.

There was once an advertisement in the Houston paper inviting the sick and needy to a week-long series of tent meetings where, it proclaimed, God would meet every need. According to a friend whose report was reliable, there were several persons who had their teeth filled through the prayers of those in charge of the meetings. Saturday morning's paper carried a huge ad of the final night's service. It boasted in large print, "Double miracles on Saturday night." And there probably were; but within the limitations of how one can judge such things, I would think that God's glory was not enhanced one farthing by that ministry.

There occurs to me another example from current history of "kingdom" events where mystery fails for lack of proper glory. Everywhere I go these days, someone is specializing in a healing gift of lengthening and strengthening uneven legs. It has become a very popular fad, performed with great flamboyance and assurance of grace. I am sure that behind the practice there stands somewhere a humble servant of Christ, through whose ministry of miraculously healing withered limbs God has been mightily glorified. Now everyone is

13

doing it and though assuredly all has been of grace in every instance where healing has been effected, my point is that seldom is it *obvious* that God is doing it. We are entering an age when the Church's witness is not so much in danger of running aground on counterfeits and imitations at the place of God's *grace* as at the place of His *glory*—for which we, as a people, have been called into being.

Americans are a pragmatic people who will try anything that works. That is one of the hidden circumstances that make the story of renewal in Redeemer Church an intricate one. The major portion of the tale covers a six-year period beginning roughly in January 1966 and is filled with miracles, dramatic healings, conversions, deliverances, and unique ministries. It is in every respect a story of outstanding success. But I have no interest in involving the parish or myself in seeing anywhere a copy of what God has done here. So my present writing is one of beginnings (a miracle story in itself) that ends when the original charismatic community was gathered together in the summer of 1965. We trusted God to rest upon our corporate shoulders the power to effect renewal throughout an entire parish, and our trust was not misplaced—but that story must wait for another telling.

My fervent prayer is that *Gathered for Power* will serve to assist in revealing the mystery of what will surely be recognized as one of America's miracle churches of the '70's; when mystery in an event of Christ's kingdom is not openly proclaimed, its miracle is no more than a spectacle. Should some other man in another time and place be called of God to survive circumstances similar to what Graham Pulkingham did between September 1963 and September 1965, then the only explanation possible would be God's grace. If after six more years' endurance a church is raised from the dust of its own dryrot into a magnificent community of love and praise, then a first-class miracle has happened—to God be the glory.

This is a story of real places and very real people. I have

told it as simply as I could, in twelve episodes touching upon its most salient features. It is a tale of ordinary folk who met in an Episcopal Church at the East-end edge of Houston's inner city. Their histories clashed or blended, but out of the colorful threads of their experience in Christ, the Spirit of God wove a fabric from which He has been fashioning a beautiful garment of praise. The present story picks up the threads and weaves the cloth.

I

No More Than A Mist
(James 4:14)

"Graham, I can't do it."

Betty looked helpless and exhausted. Her voice was flat against the street noises. Strange they should have passed by unnoticed until now; I had not been aware that our words were so intense.

Suddenly she was quiet. It was an uneasy silence and I reassured myself that her stated reasons for remaining in Austin had been given a full hearing. They had. The silence was a reflection of frustration and defeat—by now even she could tell that her reasons warranted little more than passing respect. As far as I could tell nothing remained to hinder an honest look at her fear of making such a drastic move.

Tears of resignation were flowing freely, and I kept silent letting fear define itself. When she spoke again, the edge of accusation had become bland unbelief.

"Oh Graham; Houston's not the problem. It's that church and *that* neighborhood. How could you even think of raising your children in a place like that?

"And what about me?" she complained. "Four children and one still in diapers—no yard, no parks, no family room, no playroom! Surely you realize what that means. Children upstairs. Gates at the top of the stairs. Kitchen and laundry

17

downstairs. Good gracious! And without a secretary I'll be the one who has to chase all over the place when someone thinks they need you. The phone and the doorbell will never stop. Never!"

Some of the earlier rancor had returned to her voice when, from a determined perch at the edge of the car seat, she looked me full in the face, and wide-eyed in mock defiance announced. *"I can't do it."*

The fear in her eyes was plain.

Sitting back she bowed her head and fixed her gaze on the seat between us. The wedding band caught her attention briefly before she withdrew it in haste. It was easy to discern her thoughts.

Affectionately I realized how dear she was to me, and a surge of gratitude welled up within. I wondered at my reluctance to make a verbal offering of that tenderness. Its warmth would have relieved the brittle tension of her monologue. But I remained silent.

Soon she exclaimed weakly, "A rectory right next door to the church in a place like that." There was an inarticulate moan. Then she pleaded, "Graham, couldn't we just live somewhere else? Please?"

"Listen Betty," I began firmly and with a growing sound of resoluteness. "I don't think I have a lot of choice. It seems to me that's where I belong. And besides, Bishop Hines called today. He did something I don't think he does very often; he said, 'Graham, I hope you won't betray my confidence in you, but I would like you to consider accepting the call extended by Redeemer parish.' And ... well, what can I do? I know we'll have to live in the rectory where it is, but surely we'll be able to do something, maybe add a family room. Sweetheart, we've got to go there. I'm sorry, but I can't help it."

"O God," she muttered.

It was not an ejaculation of the purest piety and I had no difficulty understanding why. Betty's glance was sweeping the graceful lawns of the capitol building. As we drove west

18

toward Austin's suburban hills, she drank in the tidy sophistication of the small city devoted to government and academic life. She had loved her years in the Texas capitol, and the latest three had been full and stimulating, crowded with fresh excitements and renewed memories of days on the University music staff. Austin had been good for her—good to her also—especially during the first two years of our marriage when she was teaching and I was in seminary. Then, after three years with the Navy in Florida, there had been one more year in Austin that ended with graduation from seminary, three years in Galveston, and three more in Austin. My imagination ticked off a list of the advantages Betty clung to: long-standing friendships at the University, the comfort of relaxed surroundings in an affluent suburb, opportunities for recreation and cultural enjoyment, excellent private and parochial schools, settled life in an established parish, a respected husband ... there was no point in continuing the list.

By way of contrast her imagination conjured up a hideous vision of life in Houston's inner city. Nor was the specter one of pure fantasy, a private vision of her own. I could easily have shared it and a moment's reflection gave me cause to wonder whether her fears were more real than I cared to admit.

The face of Houston's East End was pocked and scarred by three generations of haphazard development and growth. Comfortable middle-class neighborhoods, pockets of poverty, industrial complexes, commercial strips, all were scattered throughout the southeast sector of the city in a kaleidoscope of endless changes. The population had increased twenty-fold in little more than half a century, and from the beginning Anglo-Saxon whites had been in control. They guided the city's residential development to their own economic and social advantage. Blacks were packed together, mostly in a ring of poverty circling the downtown commercial district. Mexican-Americans, ever on the increase and occupying a major portion of the northeast urban sector, lurked north of a boundary that extended from the city's center to its circumference, and from there pushed persistently southwestward into the white establishment. Since the ethnic isolation of the Latins did not involve a sharp racial distinction, their movement across the city gave refuge at the point of meld to a class of transient poor whites. The latter were a culturally deprived group whose helpless penury classed them with the Mexicans as far as living conditions were concerned, whose lives were stuffed into meaningless clusters located on the fringe of their Mexicans neighbors' advance. And although the original settlement at Houston had been in the East End, it was that very spot—the city fathers' own backyard—which in 1963 was being most severely affected by the migrating Latins.

Nor was that all. During the 1950's Houston's blacks, trapped and restless in the squalor of their ghettos, began a radial move outward from the city's center. They progressed only a short distance, but racial barriers crumbled. Suddenly a black community on the move added impetus to the Latin American push, and the center of Houston's confused white population quickened its southwestward pace. Gracious old homes were left bleak and empty and whole city blocks were abandoned by their original white inhabitants during the span of a few years. On the city planner's map it must have looked like a game of leapfrog; in the lives of middle-class urbanites it was a frenzied flight into the safety of distant suburbs. For the blacks it was an opportunity to fill the gap.

Without ceremony, a wedge of black inhabitants thrust themselves from the center of the city due south, and a pie-shaped segment of whites became isolated between them and the encroaching Latins to the northeast. At the bite of that piece of pie stands the Episcopal Church of the Redeemer. In the beginning it was called Eastwood Community Church, named for one of Houston's gracious old neighborhoods, but that name had finally become a contradiction. An unwitting symbol of changeless wealth, it was cornered by

20

poverty in a segment of the city that was surrounded on every side except south by a population in flux.

During the '60's an urban crisis was in full bloom in Houston's East End. Thirty years earlier Redeemer Church had served an area of substantial middle-class homes. Then in its abandonment, the parish neighborhood was becoming tawdry and unkempt, an insignificant square of blocks, ten by ten, on the inner city's declining edge. There were still a few lovely homesteads whose original occupants, aged and retired—and stunned by what to them was a decade of needless dissolution—cowered behind hedgerows and bay windows like aliens. Their new neighbors, the poor whites, being driven by social forces like frightened geese before a barking dog, were condemned as culpable in their instability simply *because* they were Anglo-Saxon whites. As yet the hapless blacks and Latins a dozen blocks away were not an immediate threat. But in another ten years the few remaining oldsters would see that that, too had changed.

Betty's presence came back into focus.

She was weeping more obviously now, and I was tempted to pity her for not having found a husband more like her sedate, Southern-gentleman father.

I was tempted to be afraid too—God knows, I had never lived in a situation like that either!

While we drove, I looked appreciatively at the comfortable ranch style homes scattered among the gentle hills of Balcones Fault on the city's western limit. Austin was a special place for me, also. I found my faith there, and I found my wife there. I found my future as an Episcopal priest there too.

But Houston's Church of the Redeemer wasn't in it, I thought.

The front wheels entered our driveway and I rejected pity and fear as irrelevant. My mind was made up and I slipped into a position of unassailable conviction.

We were moving to Houston.

21

II

*An Indistinct
Sound*
(I Corinthians 14:8)

Unfortunately I had forgotten it was Friday.

Mr. Cochrane* with a great flourish had ordered shrimp, and Mr. Kearan was muttering something to the waitress about preferring snapper to shellfish. It occurred to me to change my order but then I thought, "Graham, playing games won't help a thing. These men aren't just interested in what you eat today. They want to know your habits; and you sure wouldn't eat fish on Friday if it weren't for them." So I let my stroganoff stand.

"Father," said Mr. Cochrane, over-buttering a piece of dinner roll, "you must surely appreciate the fact that the coffee hour after mass is attended by very few people. Don't you think we might eliminate that sort of nonsense? I mean, in *some* churches you would almost think the kingdom of God was meat and drink and loud conversation." His face expanded into a broad, boyish grin as he privately relished his own sarcasm.

*For self-evident reasons the names of persons in this chapter (and elsewhere when they occur in *Gathered for Power*) have been altered; the dialogue in Chapter II is a fabrication, and the circumstance is not exact history. However, the spirit and atmosphere of Redeemer Church when I first encountered it in 1963 have been faithfully recaptured in these pages.

Feeling a bit like an animal at bay, I managed a smile and hid my embarrassment behind a half-empty water glass. Conversation was painful in its awkwardness.

"I was glad to see that you prefer the *praeparatio* at the foot of the altar," said Mr. Kearan looking very serious. "I know there's a lot of talk about eliminating these old traditions but I think it's good for the people to view the priest's preparations. Any other beginning for the mass seems abrupt to me, and my devotions are really quite hindered."

Mr. Trench was nodding his head in dumb approval of everything his two friends said. He was a strange little man with an incessant grin that broadened each time I looked at him. And the broader he grinned, the redder his face became. Something about him reminded me of the Cheshire cat in *Alice in Wonderland*.

Mr. Cochrane cleared his throat several times, and leaning forward in an attitude of grave importance prepared to introduce the subject at hand. When he invited me to the luncheon he had described it as an informal gathering of interested vestrymen. Interested in becoming better acquainted with my thinking in certain matters, I think he put it. Actually, they were representative of the high churchmen, a small but vocal faction in the parish whose influence was far less than they were willing to admit, but nonetheless appreciable.

"Father," he began, "there has been a rather informal plan for Redeemer Church for some time now, and your predecessor was very much in accord with it. We thought it might be wise to lay it before you early in the time of your tenure as rector. No harm in understanding one another from the beginning is there?" He gave an embarrassed snicker, then continued after gathering his thoughts together.

"As you well know, the downtown cathedral is anything but ... well ... catholic. No slander intended you understand, but ... oh, I think you know what I mean. Houston's very large now and it's becoming more and more cosmopolitan. It seems rather a pity that catholic-minded churchmen visiting our city should be forced to worship in the unfamiliar environment of our cathedral. We've been considering for some time that since Redeemer church is only two miles from downtown—and the freeway systems being what they are, you know—we've been thinking our church might well become Houston's 'mass cathedral.' You understand the need I'm sure, Father. Several masses on Sunday and at least one each weekday for the convenience of working people. And of course appointed times for confessions too. It appears that they have never heard of *that* sacrament downtown." This time his sarcasm was without a smile.

"We consider this to be a very reasonable plan. After all, the parish is not in the kind of neighborhood where one would ordinarily expect to find a flourishing church. Most of our members come fifteen or twenty miles across town, you know. If we don't find some unique identity, it's difficult to imagine what might become of us. Or so the diocesan Department of Christian Social Relations tells us with all confidence," he taunted, tilting with a windmill of the Bishop's administration. "Frankly, I think bureaucracy in any and every form of government breeds scavengers, but they *do* seem to have a point in this matter."

The waitress bringing our food interrupted the intensity of concentration that had enveloped his friends while Mr. Cochrane addressed me. It was apparent that in their thinking a great deal hinged on my response. While we sat back allowing the waitress to rearrange dishes and set plates before us, I began to realize some of the hidden issues that had caused a fierce battle during the call of a new rector to this parish. I knew that the vote cast in favor of my name had been an uneasy seven to five, and I knew also that the vestry had struggled long in its deliberation and decision to call me. It was abundantly plain that I was not the high churchmen's man. They had lost when I accepted the call, and they were now attempting to salvage as good a peace settlement as possible.

I relaxed, uttering a noncommittal, "That's an interesting vision, Mr. Cochrane." I saw no advantage in answering questions that were as yet unasked.

The waitress finished her task and departed. After Mr. Trench's perfunctory grace—it had been spiteful of me to urge it upon him—the conversation was turned by Mr. Kearan to the memory of his mother. "She was such a great saint," he eulogized. "For years, Father, since her death, I have had a weekly requiem said for my dear mother. I wasn't a perfect son, but one day she'll see me as that, I think." His voice was quivering with emotion.

I wondered what his obsequies were hiding in his relationship to his mother. He must be almost sixty years old, I thought, and when he uses the word "mother" it sounds to me like the utterance of a pre-adolescent child. How strange—especially since he never talks of his wife, and she doesn't seem to share his profound faith.

"Of course, I'll continue the requiem," he concluded. "I trust that's convenient with you. Dr. Martin will be glad to accommodate me—his retirement income needs supplementing, you know."

"Yes, Father," said Mr. Trench, irrelevantly. "We catholic churchmen aren't very popular here in the Diocese of Texas, you know. We have to look out for ourselves, don't we? How do they say it, John? Oh yes—we are an island of orthodoxy in the midst of a sea of heresy." Mr. Trench giggled before he settled back into his silent smile.

I was still unsure of the question they were asking. Each was watching me with a very serious look of anticipation. Though I waited for a specific interrogation, none seemed to be forthcoming, so to avoid eye contact I aimlessly pushed some stroganoff from place to place on my plate.

Then Mr. Cochrane looked at me directly and said, "I'm sure you do understand what we're saying, Father. Tell me, what do you think of the plan?"

What I was thinking was far too complex for an easy explanation. Perhaps it was more that I was feeling my response instead of thinking it. Earlier in the conversation I had recalled an incident that occurred in Austin the year before and I decided to relate it to them.

"Gentlemen," I began hesitantly, "perhaps the best way I can express what I think is to tell a story. It's a simple tale, a true one that I've been reminded of often since we moved to Houston.

"Betty, you know, was a member of the choir at St. David's church in Austin. They have a fine choir, perhaps the city's best, certainly the most expensive, costing thousands a year to support. In itself, of course, that's nothing; but I had difficulty reconciling such a large music budget with the fact that St. David's spent virtually nothing to help the city's poor right at its doorstep. You see, St. David's church is in the inner city too. Since the area of my ministry was Christian Education, I didn't have to face the problem often, but every Thanksgiving and Christmas I was directly involved when the parish young people were asked to deliver food baskets to the poor.

"The thing that was so hideously plain to me was that our 'charity' was born out of our own need. Need of what? Need to do good things, I guess, because what we did was in no way related to the needs of the people we did it to. There wasn't any personal contact with them at all. And so, soon after the kids had been driven in their fathers' black limousines to deliver the baskets, the telephone started ringing: 'Come and get this basket, we want turkey not ham.' 'We don't like sweet potatoes and corn bread dressing, send sage and Idahoes.' Once a basket was returned intact with a note attached: 'Send the canned food and fruit to Mrs. Alvarez, 8th and Trinity. Have no stove to cook and don't speak English, so I write for her. She have 7 kids at home.' It was signed, 'Mrs. Sanchez.' That's sort of like the man who was unhappy about having no shoes until he saw a man with no feet. Well, the fact of a very costly music program in the

26

middle of a poverty-stricken neighborhood was more than my soul could contain quietly.

"One night after rehearsal Betty told me of an incident that summarized the whole thing for me. A 'wino'—you know, a drunk—came in off of Sixth Street and wandered into the parish hall where the choir was rehearsing. He was pretty emaciated, she said, and his breathing was labored but he didn't bother anyone—just sat and listened. At a break in the rehearsal the choirmaster turned to the man and asked him what he wanted. 'The church,' he answered. Whereupon he was informed that the church was 'over there'—the choirmaster pointed to the building next door—and was told to leave.

"I'm sure his motives were impure and I'm also sure he had just happened in from some saloon, but he was in fact looking for the church. And he was sent to an empty, cold, and dark building.

"You know, gentlemen, we can so easily be blinded by attempting to do what *our* image of the church dictates, that we miss what God has given us to do in His name. I guess that's been a problem at every church I've been a part of. It seems to me that the term 'catholic,' when you apply it to a parish, means first of all a ministry to the people and places right at its doorsteps. Why? Because the church is a creature in the middle of history, and the place where a parish finds itself is a part of the givenness of what God is saying to it. His sustaining life and word are directed to where it is. Otherwise we could publish one sermon a week and mail it all over the world. If He wanted a church to be elsewhere, He'd move it. But in that it *is* where it is, it must learn to be a servant in *that* place. Certainly the church is catholic in time, in space, and in spiritual dimension, but I think we have to remember that a catholic parish is first of all a *parish,* not a competitor of the cathedral. I think a parish that ignores the existential dimension of its time and place is no more a catholic parish than one that abandons its historic antecedents. Gentlemen, it's plain to me we have a mission, and we have a ministry. Why not get on with it? The only compelling reason not to call Redeemer Church a neighborhood parish would be that the local residents were unconvertible. Granted, the East End of Houston's not a typical Episcopal neighborhood and the people are not 'our kind' of people. But the question is not, 'are they our kind?' but 'are they Christ's?' "

"Well, Father," said Mr. Cochrane, "I can certainly admire your idealism but I must say that I can't see how to apply it to Redeemer Church. I mean, after all, parishes poach on other parishes as far away as thirty miles just to get members and meet budgets. It seems to me that you can carry the idea of parochialism too far."

I addressed myself to Mr. Kearan who seemed moved by my story. "Do you find there's much ground of agreement between yourselves and the rest of the vestry?" I asked.

Mr. Cochrane snorted an interruption. "Really, Father, surely you know vestries better than that. They don't agree on *anything*."

I changed the subject.

"I seem to miss several vestrymen on Sunday mornings. Are they still taking vacations, I wonder? Let me see, is it Winfred? And what's that other fellow's name? Ah yes, Doherty. Are they out of town?"

"Well, no," said Mr. Kearan. "Both of them live a good distance across town and ... well, I was speaking to Charlie—that's Winfred—just the other day. He's been thinking of transferring to another parish for some time. Nothing personal at all, it's just that there's been a transitional period between rectors and that seems like a good time to change. He said he had *some* uneasiness about what he was afraid your ministry might lead to, but the principal reason is that he hasn't wanted to offend Dr. Martin. You know he baptized the Winfred children and married their daughter, and it just seemed like the decent thing to do to wait until he retired. However, I'll probably see him this week again and I don't think his mind is finally made up. If I could reassure

1) Call Joe Ingle.

2) Work on newsletter: Financial pg.

3)

C: PHASE I

Year 1 (Months 1-12)									Lead Person	Rel. To Obj.*
4	5	6	7	8	9	10	11	12		
									Rog	1, 2
									Rog	1, 2
									Dennis	1
									Dennis	1
X	X	X	X	X	X	X	X	X	Rog	1
X	X	X	X	X	X	X	X	X	Dennis	1
X	X	X	X	X	X	X	X	X	Holupka	1
X		X			X		X		Dennis	1, 2
	X		X			X		X	Rog	1, 2
X		X		X			X	X	Dennis	1, 2
									Rog	1
									Rog	1
X	X	X	X	X					Dennis	1, 2
					X				Dennis	1, 2

him that you don't intend any radical changes—I don't know, he might be dissuaded. He's a valuable man, you know. Very valuable."

"What kind of changes do you think he's afraid of?" I asked.

"Oh, it doesn't matter," he said in an off-handed tone of discouragement. "Changes always upset people, I think. There are a lot of families in the parish in Winfred's position. It's not only a matter of change, it's a matter of convenience for them. Why should they go twenty miles to church when they can go ten blocks? And yet they've been doing just that for several years because, I suppose, it's easier than making a change. So you see, Father, any changes you bring about will shake an awful lot of sleeping birds out of their nests. I guess we have to expect to lose some that way."

"We already have, John" said Mr. Cochrane in a rude tone of voice. "St. Paul's, Parkplace, is doing a land office business with ex-Redeemerites! I hear they promise to get you out of church before noon so you can beat the rest of the 'prots' to the cafeteria. But what can you expect? Most of those people hung on here because of Dr. Martin. Now that he's gone, so are they."

"The parish certainly has been going downhill, Father," confided Mr. Kearan. There had been a perceptible change in his tone of voice and demeanor during the past several minutes. Until then I felt he and Mr. Cochrane were sharing with me their conclusions to speeches delivered elsewhere. Mr. Trench was still a smiling void on my consciousness— but now I felt that Mr. Kearan was sharing some real concerns. "We tried a few things to help the budget. Not much luck though. Oh, nothing desperate that we had to deal with, but a slow decline nevertheless. When Dr. Martin had his heart attack eight years ago, the doctor told him to avoid stairs, so he moved his office from the second floor of the parish building into the rectory dining room. Practically speaking, most of the parish buildings have been unused since then. We tried renting the third floor for office space

29

but it didn't work out. We don't have the custodian or the cleaning help to do the job properly."

"I never could understand why," Mr. Trench chirped nervously. "We pay two sextons to do *something*, don't we?"

"Yes, Timothy," Mr. Kearan said paternally, "but they're really there to guard the place. If we didn't have someone on the property twenty-four hours a day, the neighborhood kids would tear everything up. You see, Father, a few years ago when vandalism became a problem we let the parish secretary go and hired another sexton. You'll probably find the parish files in pretty bad shape.

"Not long ago," he continued, "I figured out that the parish property is used on the average about forty hours a month. That's not much, is it? There are very few evening meetings, you see, because people won't travel the streets in that neighborhood after dark. Sunday's about it; daytime meetings during the week aren't well attended, but there's some response."

"Let's face it, John," Mr. Cochrane interjected, "besides mass on Sunday and vestry once a month, it's the women's church. They're pretty efficient too. If we could keep them out of chasubles!"

"That's right," said Mr. Trench. "They make up our deficit budget every year."

Ignoring the question of women in the ministry, I asked, "How do they help the budget, gentlemen?"

"Oh, the annual turkey dinner and bazaar," Mr. Cochrane began to enumerate. "And they cater for Boy Scouts and Little League banquets, and the parish meeting too. Then they have card parties, bake sales, and what not. It all adds up. They're industrious, and it keeps them happy too—especially Mrs. Rector."

"Do they make contributions to the general budget?" I asked.

"Well, not exactly," he said. "Maybe sometimes they do, but for the most part they arrange to get things the vestry's vision can't afford."

"How do they manage that?" I persisted.

"Oh, Father, you know how these things work. Father Rector—or sometimes Mrs. Rector, I regret to say—makes his wishes known and, well . . . the right purchases are made at the right time."

"Such as . . . ?" I realized my questions were not only curt but uncomfortable.

"Well," said Mr. Cochrane, his cohorts having retreated behind downcast eyes and imaginary crumbs on the table-cloth, "the eucharistic vestments would be a case in point. We now have two full sets, including black, with matching altar hangings—handmade and very costly. One could scarcely expect the vestry to foot that bill, especially since things are in such a bind."

Mr. Kearan interjected almost apologetically: "Father, we had to do something about the choir program, too. You know at one time Eastwood Church choir was one of the city's best volunteer groups. There are still a few stalwart die-hards left over from those days, but you can hardly get anyone to come to rehearsal anymore so we've hired a quartet of professionals. That way you don't depend on volunteers and you always have a choir. Since the music budget amounts to about seven thousand a year—that's almost a quarter of the budget, you know—we've had to look elsewhere for some of that money. For example, I give the stipend for that good baritone who can pinch-hit for a cantor when we need one."

"Now that, I think, is far more important than serving coffee after mass," Mr. Cochrane muttered in an aside to Mr. Trench.

"Mr. Cochrane," I said pointedly, "why are you so distressed about serving coffee after mass?"

"Well, I suppose it all depends on your point of view," he blustered. "If you're going to be a happy little fellowship of people doing nice things, then you'll probably spend your money accordingly. But it seems to me we need to concentrate on the essentials."

I begged the issue of what, in his opinion, were the essentials by directing a question to Mr. Kearan.

"Mr. Kearan, have you given this stipend for a baritone in addition to your pledge?"

"Well . . . no. I guess I've adjusted my pledge a little."

"And do you think," I said testily, "this is a practice that should be encouraged among the parishioners?"

Mr. Cochrane flushed and for the first time directed his sarcasm at me. "Really Father, we're not Baptists you know, chasing after the holy tithe! I think all we're required to do is provide the essentials. Surely you're not going to spend your time chiding us for not giving enough, are you?"

"Well, not until I find out what the essentials are, Mr. Cochrane," I said as gently as I could. "But in that connection, I understand that we have difficulty paying our quota each year."

"Oh well, *that's* another matter," said Mr. Cochrane. "Not everyone on the vestry approves of Bishop Hines' policies. He seems altogether too liberal, and he has very little sensitivity to the faith. I'm not entirely sure the vestry really approves of accepting the quota, but there are some people in the parish who would be offended if we did not, consequently for the sake of Dr. Martin and a few others we usually go ahead and accept it. I'm quite sure that those who want the quota paid will find the money to pay it. I for one would not care a bit if we didn't pay it. It seems to me that we could make a good case against some of Bishop Hines' activities in East Texas. And also, you'll have to agree that the Episcopal church in the Diocese of Texas is not the greatest defender of the faith."

"Perhaps not *your* faith, Mr. Cochrane," I said icily.

"Well, Father," he drawled. "I'm sure your point of view has its merits, and when you show me a successful program of social action, I'll be glad to support it. But, reasonably now, Father, we can't expect to meet all the needs of East-wood single-handed, can we? In the meantime I'm concerned that the direction of the parish's ministry keep on in the way it's going. It seems to me the future of this parish will depend upon the kind of ministry it has, and I can't conceive of any other that would be satisfactory. I've given my full support to the parish for the past several years, and I think I can speak for Mr. Trench and Mr. Kearan at this point: Our hope is that we can serve a neglected area in the church's life in the city of Houston. Meanwhile I would certainly have to re-think my position in relation to Redeemer Church were the direction of its ministry to be altered in any significant way."

"Mr. Cochrane," I said boldly, "I can assure you I have no intention of destroying anything that's good. I was very grateful to the Senior Warden when he first approached me about accepting a call to this church. He was emphatic that the vestry had given me free rein to lead the parish in the direction of a neighborhood church. I understood from him at the time that the vestry was well aware this parish may not be eventually the kind of parish that it's been in the past, and I'm going to hold us to that. It seems to me that how people express their faith is almost a matter of indifference, just so it's the natural outgrowth of Christ among them. For us to bicker about churchmanship is to miss the point. I think the real question is who are the ones that are going to express the life of Christ among us? I hope you'll say this to your friends and to the rest of the vestry if they have any concern or wonderment about what my minstry will be. I hope to find ways of serving the neighborhood so the parish can be the servant it needs to be right where it is! That won't be an easy task—either finding the way, or bringing it to pass. I'll need all the help I can get, including yours."

III

As in a Foreign Land
(Hebrews 11:9)

I lifted my eyes from the newspaper and sniffed the air like a suspicious dog.

"Hey Betty!"

Sound from the full force of my lungs flooded the stairwell. "The coffee!"

No one answered.

I had been immersed in the religion section of Saturday's paper. It was Monday but I was grasping clumsily for the week-end news. Mondays were days when my mind moved at an elephant's gait.

In a moment the acrid aroma caught my attention again. Looking toward the newel post I bawled a sharp cadence. "Betty Jane!"

Still no reply.

Then some muffled noises from the distance reminded me that the rear of the house was beyond earshot. "Oh my, I'll be glad when they finish that family room," I thought irritably. Taking the steps two at a time I descended to the kitchen muttering wasted protests. Betty was there, huddled over the sink, and when she saw me her eyebrows raised in anticipation.

"Did you call?"

"Yes, can't you smell the coffee burning?" I chided.

Her face relaxed into a smile. "There isn't any coffee on."

"Aw, come on! What do I smell then?"

"I don't know. But it's as strong outside as it is in here. Smells like coffee—better than some things I suppose," she said off-handedly.

"Too much, it's burnt ... hmmm," I reflected, wrinkling my nose. "Those smokestacks over on Harrisburg Street must belong to a coffee plant. I heard there's one around somewhere. I guess it *is* better than the slaughter house we smelled yesterday."

Her face showed signs of agreement but she said nothing when the sudden shriek of a power saw cut painfully through the confusion of noises. With a shrug of annoyance she turned and mechanically rinsed some dishes piled by the sink.

I looked over her bent shoulders and became momentarily lost in the easy movements of workmen through the opposite doorway. They were converting a garage and storage area into a den adjoining the kitchen. The result was going to be a far better arrangement for the care of our two smallest children than the nuisance of a second-floor playroom would have been. Only because of stubborn persuasion at the first meeting I presided over, had the vestry consented to allow the change, and in the course of their deliberations an unreasoned bitterness from some of the members betrayed their real feelings about my presence in the parish. I wasn't surprised, of course, except at the pettiness and at their insensitivity to Betty's needs. Mr. Winfred's request for transfer to a suburban parish had been read earlier at the meeting, and several other members—Doherty among them—seemed uncomfortably self-conscious when Mr. Cochrane moved to accept his resignation from the vestry at the same time. I knew there was a great deal more of that sort of thing yet to come, and wondered how much of an exodus the parish would one day be forced to tolerate. However, I was by no means eager to press the issue at that moment.

35

My nostrils twitched at the pungent odor once again, and I focused my concern on Betty's tense figure.

"Did you read this?" I shouted, waving the newspaper that had been clutched under my armpit.

"Oh yes ... interesting ..." she said between spurts of the faucet, "but ... oh, I don't know, Graham ... I guess that's not my concern."

"What do you mean?" I asked with a frown. "Why shouldn't it be?"

She turned toward me, looking wan, with her eyes half closed in mute defiance of the noise. "Graham", she said slowly, "what are you going to do when all those kids show up? How in the world do you intend to keep tabs on them?"

"That's a good question," I mused almost inaudibly, wondering momentarily at my freedom to treat it like a question without cogency. I saw what a big investment I had in doing *something* for those kids, maybe even something foolish.

The strain on her nerves, drawn tight by the ceaseless construction noises from the other room, showed plainly in the purse of Betty's lips. I beckoned toward a front room where we could avoid the racket.

As we passed through a windowless, narrow hallway on our way from the kitchen to the living room, once again I shuddered at the tasteless frugality of our new home. Marvelling at the tenacity of my spirit to resist such senseless impoverishment, I knew instinctively that only an interior decorator would be able to heal the problem. The parish structures, including a two-story rectory, were all alike. They were substantial and impregnable looking with eight-inch poured concrete walls and Spanish-tile roofing that gave final touches of institutionalism. Since the rectory was a home, a family dwelling in continuous use from the outset, it might have been reprieved from the lifeless aura and impersonality of the public buildings. Who knows who was responsible for their design—it could well have been the improbable fruit of some committee's efforts. They were drab and forbidding.

Unfortunately the rectory bore the same stamp on its inner parts. The interior was dingy and worn with dark, ceiling-high wood panels and steel-grey carpeting. Hardware and electrical fixtures in every room were heavy and commercial looking, and the decorator's brush, lavish with the use of a greenish-gilt accent, had managed to create an illusion of antique elegance. Everything was dark-toned and reminiscent of the smoking lounges in Victorian men's clubs. I could almost smell the cigars. Scattered incongruously here and there was a meager array of contemporary furnishings brought by us from Austin, and seeming about as much at home as egg crates in a casket factory. The over-all effect was an indescribable sense of poverty, a poverty of humanity utterly distasteful to me and conjuring up buried memories of my religious upbringing in Canada. Nurtured under the rigid shadow of Irish Catholicism, I learned connotations to the words 'church' and 'holy' that spoke more of dust and decay than of sanctity. And with a pejorative use of those words I thought of our new home. "Church people live here." Admittedly, for most, childhood training is not sung to so bleak a religious tune as my impressionable young ears listened to under the tutelage of priests and nuns, but few have failed to experience somewhere the oppressive tyranny of this sort of Puritan impoverishment.

As we entered the living room I stifled a surge of revulsion and reminded myself that it was a sensible house after all, it was moderately comfortable and without ostentation. But I was not convinced. "Sensible," I thought, "like old-fashioned clothes are sensible to a prude."

Entering the living room, we settled in front of its mock fireplace. I lit Betty a cigarette and for a moment watched sinuous threads of smoke collide with their image in the enormous mirror over the mantelpiece. The living room was cool as well as quiet, and Betty relaxed with her eyes closed and her head bowed. She was aimlessly gathering dampened bits of hair from the nape of her neck.

The newspaper was spread on the coffee table before us

and the article's sub-captions caught my scanning eye: "Declining East End Parish Seeks New Life ... Facilities Open to Neighborhood Youth ... 'Church Must Serve Surrounding Community,' New Rector Says." It was a good feeling to see myself and the parish in print.

Wondering how the reporter first got wind of what we were doing I said, "Looks like *someone's* interested in this section of town. At least the *Chronicle* is concerned enough to publish an article about what we're trying to do."

"Seems that way," she muttered, "but I honestly don't see what all the fuss is about. So a few kids come here instead of the 'Y.' What's that anyway? Is it such a big thing?"

"Oh Betty!" I said, struggling against impatience. "Who knows at this point? But *I* can reach kids better if they're here instead of at the 'Y.' "

"Suppose so," she said casually.

I wondered why her casual air seemed such an insult to me. Avoiding a temptation to withdraw in silence I continued the conversation.

"Last night it wasn't just a few kids, though. More like a few hundred. About eleven o'clock a bunch came in off Harrisburg. They were as bad as anything I've ever seen— leather jackets, tight jeans, sideburns, shifty eyes. Didn't talk much except to whisper to each other ... just walked around and made everyone uncomfortable." I stopped talking for a moment and stared into the fireplace, remembering their insolence with astonishment.

"When I stuck out my hand to one of them he curled his lip and walked away with a girl giggling in his ear. And do you know what those kids call me? They say, 'Hey priest!' Not 'Hey Father,' but 'Hey priest.' How do you like that?"

Betty's eyes were still closed but she responded with an imperceptible snort and a smirk.

Her detachment seemed to be more than simple preoccupation with heat and humidity. The unused cigarette burned in an ashtray, and while I was speaking she repeatedly pressed the same few wisps of wayward hair into the up-swept pile on her head.

"About midnight," I continued, "things got quiet in the pool room, so I went down to see what was happening in the gym. It was bedlam—completely out of hand. Mostly young-sters, too, not the older bunch. About a hundred of them running around, screaming, pushing, things flying every-where, clothes torn off their backs! They're no more inter-ested in organized sports than I am in sniffing glue."

"Sniffing glue!" she said with exaggerated contempt. "What's that?"

"Oh, they take airplane glue—you know, the kind that comes in model kits. They squeeze it into a paper sack and put it over their noses, then they inhale the fumes. It makes them high, like liquor. Sometimes they walk along the street with a wash rag soaked in the stuff—looks like they're in another world. Twelve-, fourteen-year-old kids, wandering around in a daze, dreamy and stupid with radios plugged in their ears and sacks at their noses!"

I experienced a mild tremor of revulsion while I thought about it.

"Anyway," I went on, "the gym was a shambles and smelled like a banana stand. I couldn't shout loud enough to make myself heard, so I turned off the lights and waited. They got tired of screaming and bumping into each other and finally left, a few at a time. About one o'clock I chased the last one out."

"I can't *believe* that." Betty's detachment had vanished and her voice was raised to a pitch of incredulity. "Graham, this is Monday, a school day. Don't they go to school? Who looks after them anyway?"

Her face registered an unmistakable disdain.

"Some went to school," I said vaguely. "Mostly truants and dropouts, though . . .."

Even I caught the tone of distraction in my own voice. I was troubled. All during our conversation there had been a storm brewing in me. It was difficult to understand why a response such as Betty was making to our new neighbors' lifestyle made me be so defensive. Yet defensive I was; and I was frustrated because not one shred of their behavior could be endorsed by a dispassionate observer as productive or even necessary.

I wondered what was happening to me. *Getting soft,* I thought, *or more likely, too involved to be rational.*

But here was my position: several parishioners, concerned and well-intended upright citizens, had cautioned me that these children were incorrigible, coming from 'hard-core' situations for which there was no relief. 'Hard-core' was a social-work term used by one parishioner to describe families who breed children and welfare problems indiscriminately. She was a county worker laboring among those who receive Aid to Dependent Children, and she was one of the more vocal examples of the parish's despair. Her judgments were not condemnatory, they were simply an assessment of fact from her point of view. She was convinced that those youngsters would be doing their very best if they could avoid serious trouble long enough to marry and beget their own brood of public charges.

What am I defending? I asked myself. *Not their behavior, certainly not their point of view. But under all of that crap there's a person. I guess it's just them—they themselves—I feel so protective of.* I was amazed at my own feelings.

I'm actually attracted to those kids, I thought. *I'd like to go with them wherever they call home, and I'd like to see them while they eat and sleep and dress and laugh and cry and whatever else they do in the course of a day's living. I'd like to be with them away down inside beneath the callousness and hostility and aggression; I'd like to live in their skin for awhile. I wonder if I'd make it?*

I suppose my disturbance at Betty's response was rooted in the overwhelming sense of hopelessness I felt. I had never expressed it verbally to anybody, but my thoughts were almost bitter with the weight of it.

Imagine a middle-class, white, Anglo-Saxon parish mak-

ing significant contact with either these kids or their parents! Ha! Oh, we'll send them a little money, or a professional who will try and do some kind of good for them, but the only thing that's going to help these people is a 'live-in' situation—some daily sharing with wholesome lives that aren't troubled like theirs are.

Take Ronny for example. Ronny's mother's a whore. And the only reason he doesn't call her that, the way he does all the others that are like her, is because he calls her 'Mom!' It's that simple. And, of course, he doesn't even know who his dad is.

And Rueben. His folks don't speak English at all. Who knows what goes on at their house? Blinds never raised, votive lights in every room, statues, strange smells, and too many kids! How can you force on the Ronnys and Ruebens the same standards you apply to my children, and then come up with a question like "who looks after them?" No one does. There hasn't been anyone looking after them since they were ten. "Bread 'n mustard tastes as good as hot dogs," one twelve-year-old was heard grumbling to his sister who asked him why he hadn't been home for meals in several days. "And ya' don't need no mouthy old lady to put mustard on a piece of bread, neither."

I had assumed, charitably, since my uneasy parishioners now lived across town—many had been raised within a stone's throw of the church but had long since moved—that they were too far from the East End to see the situation for what it really was. Of course, the distance factor was not true of everyone. A small cluster of oldsters who had retired to live out their days in nearby homes where their families had been raised (and where their hearts had been transplanted many years ago) made up a significant cadre of the fearful. Though residents, they were neighborhood misfits who seldom ventured past the garden gate except when fetched by their children. Occasionally they sallied forth into shops and church, but mainly they were just idling away the remainder of their days.

41

I realized that such generalizations about my charges were not universally applicable, but there was enough evidence as far as I was concerned to warrant the conclusions being drawn. One thing had become abundantly clear to me—whether you live across town or not, "across town" can live in you. Betty had been right here in the midst of things, living in it and walking in it almost as much as I. And even though she was attempting to understand, her response was little different from that of the rest of the parish. I was finding it impossible to pretend any longer that Houston's east and west ends shared a common world in any but the most superficial ways. Chief among the confusions was a fact that posed a plaguing question: How could any but the unscrupulous have frequent contact with the parish neighborhood and remain aloof to its contradictions?

Surely Betty sees the disparity, I thought, *the school across the street ... untidy, empty playgrounds, cracked windows ... the ancient equipment in those steamy classrooms ... poorly clad children clinging to their slatternly mothers; and the filthy rags on those kids in Goodwill buggies ... fingers and cheeks streaked with dirt clinging to the drivel of endless confections. She's seen the second- and third-rate merchandise in local stores, the exhorbitant cost of wilted produce and cheap cuts of meat. She's seen dump heaps for yards and dilapidated houses covered with scribbled obscenities. She's seen things right across the street that she never dreamt existed!*

By what fair standard do you judge the product of poverty and deprivation? my wrath-filled soul demanded. And yet in spite of every defense, what those kids do is vicious and mean and destructive. *What reasonable man could deny it?* I moaned.

The mute tirade was drowned in a flood of discouragement, and I sighed.

Finally I spoke, trying to sweeten the sound of bitterness.

"You know, Betty, whether they're in school or not isn't the biggest issue in these kids' lives. Remember the little freckle-faced girl named Mary, the redhead who hangs around so much?"

"Yes, I sure do. The child I was talking with after church yesterday?"

I nodded assent.

"Poor thing," she continued. "Never did get to Sunday school, you know. Not because she wasn't on time, either, but no one told her what to do or where to go, so she wandered around the church till after noon. She looked so strange, poor child, clean—but her dress! It was at least two sizes bigger than she was, and the hem hanging down in the back!"

"That's the girl," I inserted quickly. "Last night when I left the gym she was sitting outside under a street light. I asked her why she didn't go home and she said her mother works until three. She doesn't like to be home alone so she roams the streets till her mother gets in. Three A.M., imagine that! Twelve years old, I suppose. Said she has an older brother but he's never home."

Betty's mouth fell open in honest amazement as I continued. "I asked her about the rest of the family. But she said there were just the three of them. Then she said the strangest thing. Listen to this: she figures she could've had several brothers and sisters, but her mother keeps giving them out for adoption when she goes to the hospital to have them. I couldn't resist asking her when was the last time that had happened. She said she's going back to the hospital to have another one soon—said she looks big enough already, but they don't have enough money to keep this one either."

"What in the world does her mother do?" Betty asked slowly, gazing distractedly past me at some private vision my words inspired.

"Ha!" I ejaculated unkindly. "You mean where does she do it? Mary said she works in a bar run by one of her men friends. I think that's what she called him."

"Oh Graham. That makes me feel just awful." Betty's voice was soft and resonant with feeling. "The reason I spent

43

so long with her yesterday was because I found her alone in the choir room. Pathetic little figure, bent over the piano and picking out hymns with one finger. She wanted to know if she could come there today after school. I hated to tell her it was locked all the time. But that's a very good piano, you know, and the wrong use would ruin it in a hurry. I wish I had time to give her lessons. How very, very, sad . . ."

Suddenly the telephone in the hallway jangled. After the second ring, when I didn't move, Betty rose to answer it. I heard her musical, "Hello," and listened to see if it was for me.

"Yes, this is his residence," she said. "This is Mrs. Pulkingham speaking."

I could tell by the tentative note in her voice that something was up.

As I rounded the corner and came into view she gave me a wide-eyed and shocked look of amusement. With a gesture she stopped me where I was. Then her humor changed to an angry accusation.

"That's a terrible thing to say," she sputtered. "I should think the least you might do is come and see him yourself."

"My dear, since you won't give your name, I see no reason why I . . ."

"Well I'm sorry you feel that way, but everything he said is true." There was a pause and Betty listened intently with her brow furrowed.

"I have nothing to say to you about that matter," she said with finality.

"No, nothing."

"Are you sure you won't leave your . . .?"

She gave a sudden blink and frowned at the earphone. "Hung up on me," she explained, replacing the receiver.

"What was her trouble?" I asked.

"The newspaper," said Betty superfluously.

"I could tell that. But what about it?"

Still scrambling for some lost composure, Betty speculated

idly on her way back to the living room, "I don't see how she had the nerve to do that. What was to be gained?"

"Do what?" I insisted impatiently, following her.

"Well," she hesitated. "It seems she and her husband have bought a house near here, one of those old big ones, and they've put a bunch of money into it. I guess they thought it would be cheaper than building one out in the suburbs. Anyway, she said she's been talking to lots of the old residents in this neighborhood and they agree that your coming to this church was a very big mistake. She says Dr. Martin was a kind man who didn't bother anybody and all you're doing is upsetting people. Even your parishioners think that. Graham, she's just a crank."

"What else did she say?" I pressed.

"Well ... Oh Graham. She said they think there's something 'funny' about you, having to hang around those kids who don't belong here anyway. Said you're just trying to make a name for yourself, putting all that stuff in the paper, and all you're doing is 'telling lies and ruining property values,' to quote her. She said everyone around here is going to stop going to this church because of you."

I felt a chill of anxiety.

"A-a-aw," I growled, wondering where the attack might come from next. "Too bad she wouldn't leave her name," I said soberly. "But I don't suppose it would do much good to talk to her anyway."

A clatter in the hallway heralded the children's return from school. In a moment Bill, our eldest, poked his head in the living room to say blandly, "Daddy, some boys want to see you outside."

Betty had been much more concerned about the recent apathy in Bill's responses than I had, but lately there was a pronounced listlessness about everything he did. Where he had always been a quiet child, judicious in temperament, suddenly—actually since our move—he was withdrawn. I hoped he could handle the shock of moving from the highly stimulating environment of St. Andrews School in Austin to

45

one of Houston's poorest public schools; suddenly someone had painted his entire world cold and grey. "He'll make it," I reassured myself, whether reasonably or not.

As I stepped from the front doorway, two local junior high drop-outs appeared from behind a tall hedge. They were both named Bobby.

"Hi, Bobby," I said, looking from one to the other. "What's up?"

"Yeh, priest," the taller one said giving his buddy a shy little grin. "We need to see a doctor. Y' know a good 'un? Cheap?"

"Well, yes. But why do you need a doctor?" I probed.

"Well, we figger we got this here problem he can help us with."

"What's the problem?" Neither of them had looked me in the eye since we began talking, so I was anticipating their meaning.

"Okay, okay," the small one snapped. "So we got the 'clap.' You wanna help us?"

"Sure," I said quietly. "But how do you know that's what you've got? Both of you got it?"

I was trying to find out who they got it from, but they thought I was asking about symptoms.

"Yeh," said the taller one, cupping his crotch with his hand. "There's this kinda hot feeling up inside me, and it keeps drippin' a green sticky stuff on my shorts. That's what we got all right." He grinned, whether from pride or embarrassment, I wasn't sure.

"You've had it before?" I queried.

"Yeh."

"Get it the same place?"

"Reckon so."

"Who is she? Do you know her name?"

"Aw come on. Get off it, priest."

"No, I'm serious."

"That ain't fair."

"Come on now, I need to know."

"Okay. But it won't do you no good. It's that little fat pig, Jean. She hangs around them empty apartments down the street—you know, the burnt out ones. Back doors are wide open, and they got beds and mattresses left in there. She's passin' it out all the time to them foreign sailors off Harrisburg. Sometimes she helps us out. She's Okay. Man she's a hog about it, though."

"What can we do for her?" I offered.

"Nothing. You can't help her, priest. Listen, she's been puttin' out since she was twelve. Her old man'll take care of her. He don't care what she does jus' so she don't get knocked up again. Don't waste your time. Okay?"

"She's had kids?" I asked.

"Nah. Abortions. Hey, ya gonna help us?"

"Let me make a phone call," I said, turning toward the house.

I looked up the number of the Eastwood Clinic on our emergency list by the phone and dialed. While waiting for someone to answer my thoughts caught me up short. "My God, she's about fifteen and so are they. Three years older than Bill—and our Mary's only a year behind him! My own kids, with dozens of youngsters headed in just the same direction as these three! Good God, what that could mean."

"Clinic," came melodically from a professional-sounding voice across the wire.

"Dr. Elliot, please. Tell him Father Pulkingham's calling."

"Dr. Elliot has transferred his practice to the Southpark Clinic, Father. You should have been notified that your records have been transferred too. You can reach him there."

I recalled seeing a post card notice that I hadn't bothered to read.

"Will he not practice at Eastwood any longer?"

"No, sir. This clinic is closing down next month. But Dr. Elliot will certainly want to take care of you and your family still."

"But what about the rest of the neighborhood?" I interrupted, recalling a poignant picture of the clinic's waiting room. It was always crowded with wide-eyed and pasty children cowering behind parents rendered mute and sullen by poverty.

"I don't know. You'll have to talk to the doctors about that," she concluded.

"What's the number down there?" I asked, feeling forsaken and sensing that familiar flutter of anxiety again.

I dialed the number and while waiting for the second call to be answered, I watched the boys out the front door. They were sitting on the steps facing the street. Relaxed like that, they looked from behind like little children, their silhouettes seemed soft and needy.

Something gentle and tender moved in my breast as I stared at them.

IV

... *A God in Heaven Who
Reveals Mysteries*
(Daniel 2:28)

*I didn't know Alliene
and Wiley Vale a few hours ago when they picked me up for
dinner, and here I am sitting in the back seat of their car
blubbering like a baby.*

My thoughts were engulfed in darkness. We had parked
and the street light illuminated only a portion of the front
seat.

*Tears streaming down my cheeks ... no use trying to hide
them, even though it's dark, not with all the grunts and
sucking sounds I've been making ... I wonder what's going
on in me anyway—release of tension? ... Possibly. This
weekend's been like a fantasy trip in a Capote novel.*

We sat in silence for several minutes during which my soul
guieted and became more reflective. Glancing across the
street in the direction of the church, I saw the soft nightlight
from a second floor hallway shining on the cloister roof.

*That would be an excellent spot to climb up and break
into the building, wouldn't it?*

I made a mental note to check the inside window latches
tomorrow.

*These Vales, they're sweet people ... quiet and cultured.
He's an architect and she's a decorator. Talented, too.*

Too comely silhouettes in profile facing each other, heads

49

resting against the car doors, were clearly defined in front of me. I studied them appreciatively for a while.

It must have been Grace Murray, one of our stalwarts, who set them on my trail. I'm glad. They're good people ... and that was a good seafood place they took me to tonight ... Walker's in Kemah, right on the waterfront. Wow, I wish it had been warm out ... I'd have enjoyed the sea breezes for awhile. Oh well, it was a good evening anyway....

Imagine what Alliene must have gone through ... taking two psychopathic kids into her home, hoping money and kindness could straighten them out. About as goofy as me thinking a church could change a neighborhood just by a little attention and concern. Guess it would be worse right in your own home though ... kids who lie, steal, and cheat, make empty promises day after day. That'd be hard to live with. You can tell she really loved them too. Boy, it must have torn her up to turn them over to the detention home for keeps—sorta like me closing the church again, only worse, I suppose.

But what about this Wilkerson fellow and the Teen Challenge place he runs in Brooklyn? That really got me. I've never cried like that before ... like someone turned on a spigot—all of a sudden bloop! And there I was ... blubbering.

Imagine! Kids like the ones around here—and worse— turn to him for help. He asks God to help them and God helps them—just like that ... Unreal! That's too good to be true.

It never occurred to me to turn the whole thing over to God. How could it be that simple? Yet Wilkerson's prayers are doing what we couldn't do with all our concern and good intentions. That's what Alliene said, and I've no reason to doubt her.

A line from a Browning poem strolled across my mind: ... think, Abib; dost thou think? So, the All-Great, were the All-Loving too——

Think, Graham! ... dost thou?

I was too drained—weak and fuddle-neaded. I didn't want to do any more thinking, so I bade the Vales goodnight and told them I'd see them again soon ... and I meant it. As I crossed the street to the rectory, memories from the past three days revived the shudder of dread in my soul. *It started with that opening service for the Junior High workshop on Friday night. ...*

I guess that's the last time the diocese will ask to have a workshop in my parish. Wasn't trying to shock anyone, but they asked me, "How can we help a church in a changing neighborhood?" So I asked them back, "What principles of Christian education would be meaningful to a fourteen-year-old kid who makes his pocket money hustling homosexuals on the city streets?" Boy, they were hostile, but I wasn't baiting them. I wanted to know because I've got a handful of youngsters who fit that category. It seems to me a whole new concept of youth ministry's needed—I don't know how to reach those kids. I don't reckon anybody does.

Then Saturday was really uncomfortable. Those very kids wandering all over the place ... poking their faces in the displays, laughing and running through the halls. Couldn't have been any more obvious that the Department of Christian Education's geared to upper middle-class kids. What a farce to have their workshop in our end of town!

Sunday morning's the nasty one though. Linda was hysterical when they took her home. Gosh it's hard to predict what those kids'll do; Larry's been like a frightened bird everywhere I've seen him—sullen and cowed. Whoever sent him to the seventh grade class must have been out of his head. Sure he's in the seventh grade, but how old is he—Sixteen? ... maybe he's retarded, I don't know, but he's still in school. I'll bet it took all the guts he had to go into that classroom ... I can see it now: the teacher was probably more scared than he was. But why in the world would he light up a cigarette in class? That crazy kid! I suppose he figured the whole thing wasn't worth it anyway. But she should've let him alone instead of trying to force him out when he wouldn't quit smoking. I can see why he slapped her across the room, but she'll never understand. I'm sure that was an ugly bruise on her face, too. . . .

While undressing for bed I mulled over the evening's conversation. Thoughts of Dave Wilkerson and Teen Challenge kept returning.

Once in bed, sleep came quickly as the words of Browning's poem transported me into oblivion:

. . . Think, Abib; dost thou think? So, the All-Great, were the All-Loving. . . .

A week later the vestry's decision was unanimous to close the church doors once again, their unanimity arose out of common despair in the face of an overpowering enemy—the neighborhood. During the seven months since my arrival as rector, the parish had lost about seventy-five families whose commitment, though small, had at least helped sustain the financial base of a faltering corporate life; four vestrymen and twelve thousand dollars in pledges vanished among them. With income and leadership thus reduced by one-third, the vestry entered the doldrums; there was no visible hope of our rescue. During the previous fifteen years two other Episcopal parishes, two Methodist congregations, one Baptist and one Disciples of Christ church had fallen victim to the same relentless pattern of change sweeping across the city's face. We were next in line. Apparently there remained nothing for the vestry to do but share dispirited opinions about how to avoid the neighborhood onslaught or where to solicit funds for some new programs to keep enthusiasm pumped up. Parish ranks were so decimated by withdrawals that even budget squabbles seemed senseless. Human need of the most desperate kind was all around, but what to do about it and how to go about doing it had escaped them entirely.

For my own part I shared their confusion and gloom, and most of the time I lived on the edge of despair. My family had been torn from its middle-class comforts and the children still showed signs of trauma; Betty looked haggard and worn; my investment of everything, personal and professional, had failed.

Escape was not impossible, though. Appeal to the Bishop for relief or the intervention of friends in another diocese might well have produced a call to minister on safer ground, but something unpredictable had happened in my soul; the thought of escape was as unbearable as the thought of remaining. I was being driven from within, compelled by an unaccustomed force of compassion. All of my attention, my feelings, and my interest came to bear on a complex of woes, the victims of which had become the chief object of every pastoral concern I had. And the vestry could close the doors to the church and rail bitterly against the vandals and ne'er-do-wells who seemed to be at the hub of our parish crisis, but I couldn't close the doors to my heart, nor did I want to. I was like a man with a new love.

Yet the decision to close the church was a relief. The past several months of my life had been a merry-go-round whirling at a giddy speed. Hordes of troubled youngsters and other torn samples of humanity had been jumping on and off at every hour of the day and night. Efforts to help them had been fruitless and, if anything, their condition was worsened by the experience of another failure. I was bone weary. Locking the chuch doors had silenced the noisy calliope in my soul and slowed the machinery to a halt, but disappointment and disillusionment could now begin to have their full effect.

That was early Lent, 1964. When the vestry that made that decision adjourned, I waited impatiently for the men to leave, feeling strangely as though I had an appointment with sorrow. I was thoroughly disheartened. Finally, alone, I went to the seldom-used chapel in the basement and wept.

Thereafter there were frequent nightly intrusions from neighborhood youths—some were vandalous, most were only mischievous—but now the buildings were officially closed, empty and tomb-like except for a few hours each week when public services were held. The church property was in the same dormant condition it had been in when I arrived the September before with one notable exception—it was defaced and in some places destroyed beyond repair. With increasing frequency I sat alone in the chapel weeping, consumed with grief—a grief encompassing neighborhood, family, and church.

It seemed that everything was lost. Despite that, however, my soul would not tolerate the idea that the gospel had failed to bring healing in these desperate lives. And in the chill of a cellar retreat I responded in fury to my feelings of desolation and abandonment, accusing God of trickery in his dealings with human suffering. Day by day my ears accustomed themselves to emptiness, listening to the incessant hum of the chapel's flourescent lights as I strained for answers to my questions. Only sobs punctuated the hollow sound of despair. Shaking an angry fist at the God of this dilemma, I demanded to know the cause of my failure. If He heard, I was not aware. Silence was His only answer.

As weeks passed, loneliness and dread began to settle upon me like a fog. Soon there were timorous pleas for help displacing the inquisitions, and a disconsolate soul cried out for comfort. I had begun by requiring of God that He explain His indifference to my failure; I had come round to the place of longing to hear just a word. Once during a moment of meditation, a Bible on the pew seat caught my attention. Opening it at random, I heard the voice of Job utter my complaint:

> I cry to thee and thou dost not answer me; I stand, and thou dost not heed me.
> Thou hast turned cruel to me; with the might of thy hand thou dost persecute me.
> Did not I weep for him whose day was hard? Was not my soul grieved for the poor?
> My heart is in turmoil, and is never still; days of affliction come to meet me.

(Job 30:20–21, 25, 27)

There came an imperceptible moment in Eastertide when my mood changed, and through the gloom shone a faint flicker of light. Two incidents that had been forgotten until then crept into my consciousness; they had been occasions of sharing and communion that happened under circum- stances at least as improbable as the present one. Their details were never very clear and whether they were remem- bered exactly, I was not sure, but they stood out in stark relief against the surrounding disillusionment.

After my second year in seminary I had worked for the summer in Austin's State School for the feeble-minded. In one of the compounds for severely retarded children there was a ten-year-old boy named Garcia. He was a surprisingly beautiful child with almost perfect Castilian features, the only sign of affliction being a peculiar cast to his eyes. Garcia had never spoken an intelligible word in his life, and from infancy his most primitive functions had to be attended to by others. He was uneducable. The days of his lonely and meaningless existence were spent pacing aimlessly from cor- ner to corner of the compound with his hands tied behind his back. There were fettered because of self-destructiveness. I was told that he had to be watched carefully for a pattern of behavior that began with a gentle rock and a hum. As it progressed, I was told, the rocking would become agitated and the humming an angry chant, until eventually he would throw himself to the ground in violent spasms and pummel the earth with his head.

Physical restraint was found to be the only effective mea- sure of prevention, and I was shown a long leather thong with which to tie Garcia to an upright chair should the behavior begin in my presence.

One day I was seated on the attendant's perch overlooking the compound, and Garcia was standing directly beneath me slowly shifting his weight from foot to foot, oblivious to his surroundings. I heard the strange humming sound. It was not meaningless to my ear however, but was a familiar musical phrase. Searching my memory I realized it sounded like the beginning of a hymn tune, actually the first half of its first phrase—six notes in all. *Surely every child has hummed those very notes at some time,* I thought. *They're so simple—the childlike sound of an Irish folk tune. But it's the beginning of a hymn called "Slane."* Garcia was humming the phrase over and over again and becoming louder with each repetition. *Was he really singing part of a folk tune? Incredible!* I waited and at the right moment hummed six more notes to finish his phrase. The boy stopped abruptly and cocked his head listening for a moment before he began chanting again. Leaning forward I interrupted him and finished the phrase once more. He stopped. Rising, he turned to look in the direction of the sound though he avoided my glance. Then he walked away subdued.

I waited several days before a second opportunity presented itself. When again Garcia began his quiet hum, I managed to approach unnoticed and supplied the second half of the unfinished phrase. Again the accustomed course of behavior was averted and he walked away quietly. Not long after that a third occasion arose. This time I sang considerably more of the tune after the finished first phrase brought him to silence. He looked at me—or so it seemed. Our eyes did meet! Was there really an open sharing in that glance? After a moment he turned away, but deep within I knew our souls had touched in that moment.

My summer employment at the State School was interrupted by the premature birth of our first child in North Carolina where Betty had gone to be with her mother. Before leaving Austin I looked into Garcia's record. Though meager, it was revealing.

The violent self-destructiveness was a recent development beginning a few years earlier when his foundling blanket had been destroyed for sanitary reasons. He had been left in a large Texas city by an Irish mother who had traveled to the United States with her illegitimate son in search of his father. The child was born in Ireland, presumably shortly after the father was repatriated during the Second World War. When he had been abandoned, he was less than two years old and appeared to be normal. Left in a basket on the steps of a church, he had a note pinned to his swaddling blanket: "Please, someone, I have failed. Find Sergeant Juan Garcia, he lives somewhere in Texas. Take the child to him, he is his father. I cannot stay here alone any longer, and I must not take the baby home without a father. May God forgive me." There was a scribbled signature above the printed word "Dublin." The mother had returned to Ireland.

The connection between this incident and the following one was not plain to me, but the two appeared in my conscious memory as parallel events.

Several years after graduation from seminary I came face to face for the first time with some spiritual healers among members of a prayer group in St. David's Church, Austin. As I watched their behavior from a distance, my opinion of them grew negative in the extreme. They were over-emotional enthusiasts whose fanatical claim of miracles, I insisted, was unnecessary. I was convinced that the God of creation was not so capricious as to worry about hangnails while winking at the fact of war and human misery. A greater miracle, I averred, was the introduction into history of powers for reconciliation, a ministry resting in men's hands. My hold upon this opinion flew in the face of fact, unfortunately. More often than not their hangnails were healed, and my reconciling work was hidden.

Once while the Rector was vacationing, I fell heir to conducting the Thursday morning prayer group and healing service, and it made me very uncomfortable. The members of the group were individually very dear to me, but during those meetings they displayed a freedom to participate that caused me to feel uneasy, so I called it license; their abandonment to worship alarmed me, because I saw it as excessive.

One weekday morning I encountered a member of the prayer group coming up the front steps of the church as I

57

was descending to the street. She greeted me almost coyly. "The Lord be with you." My good humor was aroused and I gaily replied, "And with thy Spirit." With which she halted and said soberly while bowing her head and folding her hands, "Let us pray." Irreverently I blurted my astonishment, "You must be kidding! In front of God and all these people out here?" There was no prayer. I blustered down the steps in red-faced embarrassment and did not look back.

Taking the occasion of the prayer meeting to teach them that morning, I filled the hour with a lesson on Christian responsibility. However, during the Eucharist that followed, I heard a commotion in the nave, and looking up saw a group of Latin Americans enter the church and join the worshippers. I identified them as fundamentalists or Pentecostals because from the time of their arrival the liturgy was peppered with ejaculations of praise. None of their faces was familiar to me, though. After the benediction I went among the people to introduce myself and discovered the late-comers were from an Assembly of God church; most of them were Mexican nationals conducting revivals in Austin's Spanish-speaking east end. They had come to the service to investigate charismatic healing gifts among Episcopalians. Hearing that I thought, *How unfortunate, they came on the wrong day.*

When I was introduced to the evangelist in charge of the group it was through his interpreter that I learned he had been a chaplain with Castro's rebel forces in Cuba; the man himself spoke only Spanish. My interest was piqued. I had no idea Castro was even tolerant of the Christian religion, so I invited the evangelist and his interpreter to accompany me to my study in the quiet of an adjoining building.

Our conversation was lengthy, forty-five minutes in all, and during the whole of it I was rapt in attention to the Cuban's story. He told me that he and Castro were raised in the same neighborhood and were the children of poor parents from a Catholic background. When they were boys an itinerant preacher came through town, and both of them were converted to the evangelical persuasion. Beginning then, he related, both he and Castro carried the breast pocket New Testaments that had been given them by the preacher. The man spoke bitterly of Roman Catholic persecution of Protestants, and of the Church's share in oppressing the poor. He had lost contact with Castro for a while during the time of his Bible training but had returned to join his childhood friend at a guerilla retreat in the mountains of Oriente. He discovered that Castro's interest had turned from the social teachings of Jesus to the doctrine of Karl Marx, and it was apparent that communism was becoming the rebel's religion. The young chaplain returned home, and when Castro's forces took over the government he fled to Mexico. Since then, he had been traveling into Texas conducting revivals among Spanish-speaking Americans.

When we finished our conversation the interpreter commented, "I didn't know you Episcopalians had the gift of tongues." His words filled me with alarm and I hastily retorted, "I didn't either." Then he pointed out that from early in our conversation I had been speaking English and the other Spanish, and the intensity of communication was such that we had no need for his services—we had bypassed the interpreter! In retrospect I realized with astonishment that what he was saying was true, and I knew I did not understand Spanish. He assured me that the Cuban spoke no English but that God had enabled us to understand each other. I was amazed.

One Saturday shortly after Easter I was pacing the confines of my small office while preparing a sermon on I Peter, chapter two. In tears, I accused myself of hypocrisy, and demanded, *Graham, how can you stand before these people and talk about the delivering power of Christ when the need is plain and nothing ever happe. s? Every day the broken and the torn parade through here and you have nothing to offer but empty words and a little money.* In the midst of my peevishness and tears I thought, *When will God weary of*

59

hearing my cry, and answer me or take away this burden and set me free?

The weeping stopped when my conscious mind was unexpectedly overwhelmed with an irrational conviction in the form of two short words: "Stop smoking."

I tried to dismiss the thought, but it came back with greater force.

Stop smoking, indeed! I thought.

Had the words not been impressed upon me with such authority I would have laughed aloud. *What had my smoking to do with the need of this neighborhood for deliverance from its squalor? Was God capricious after all? Would He tinker with petty moralisms when confronted by human suffering?* For three days I parried with that command, but could not be rid of it. Then I capitulated.

While driving home the following Tuesday night from a prayer meeting at which my favorite pipe had been strangely misplaced, I spoke to God as a man speaks to a man. *I don't know what smoking has to do with these things, but if you don't want me to smoke, then I don't want to smoke. But you'll have to do it, because you know as well as I that I can't. Why, I've never tried to stop even during Lent . . . had better sense than to try something I couldn't finish. So . . . on your say-so, I'll quit. Right now. I'll even throw the rest of this pack away. There! Now . . . you told me to quit, and I know I can't do it, so you'll have to take the habit from me and I'll never smoke again. And please, when you take away my cigarettes, heal my ulcers, too?*

I felt wildly exhilarated and pressed my foot on the gas to hurry home. I was going to throw the rest of the carton of cigarettes in the trash and take that whole shelf of antacids, barbiturates, and tranquilizers and flush them down the toilet. *I'll never need those things again,* I thought.

While driving up the Gulf Freeway on the last lap home, I registered another irrational thought. It had the same voice of authority.

Read the third chapter of Matthew.

Instead of driving in the driveway, I parked in front of the church, and went directly to my office to read.

In those days came John the Baptist, preaching in the wilderness of Judea, "Repent, for the kingdom of heaven is at hand." For this is he who was spoken of by the prophet Isaiah when he said,

"The voice of one crying in the wilderness: Prepare the way of the Lord, Make his paths straight."

Now John wore a garment of camel's hair, and a leather girdle around his waist; and his food was locusts and wild honey. Then went out to him Jerusalem and all Judea and all the region about the Jordan, and they were baptized by him in the river Jordan, confessing their sins.

But when he saw many of the Pharisees and Sadducees coming for baptism, he said to them, "You brood of vipers! Who warned you to flee from the wrath to come? Bear fruit that befits repentance, and do not presume to say to yourselves, 'We have Abraham as our father'; for I tell you, God is able from these stones to raise up children to Abraham. Even now the ax is laid to the root of the trees; every tree therefore that does not bear good fruit is cut down and thrown into the fire.

"I baptize you with water for repentance, but he who is coming after me is mightier than I, whose sandals I am not worthy to carry; he will baptize you with the Holy Spirit and with fire.

(Matthew 3:1-11)

The reading had been quick, and I devoured the words avidly. The passage stabbed at my soul as though its writing had been just for the occasion of my present need. It was uncanny. The thoughts and sentences had a clarity and openness that I had never experienced except in the context of immediate, person-to-person involvement. I could easily have substituted the phrase "Presbyterians and Episcopalians" for "Pharisees and Sadducees" and I saw in the reference to the fatherhood of Abraham a parallel to our traditionalism. But my heart responded with a gentle thrill and I knew my prayers would be answered.

I went home and rid myself of the cigarettes and medicine, and fell asleep in peace.

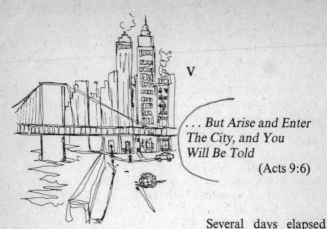

V

. . . But Arise and Enter
The City, and You
Will Be Told

(Acts 9:6)

Several days elapsed
from the night that half-empty pack of cigarettes sailed from
my car window, before I was free to announce that the habit
was gone. It was, there being not the slightest desire to
smoke, but I thought others would require a better empiri-
cism than what my simple convictions afforded. Not only
was there no desire; but the taste, the addictive hunger, and
signs of withdrawal were entirely absent too, and my faith
was enormously strengthened. However, when the news
spread there was some irrational opposition. For reasons
that escape me, non-smoking has become one of the cultural
symbols associated with biblical fundamentalists. A pentecostalist who takes up smoking is in no greater difficulty
than an Episcopalian who by simple conviction quits. So in
some quarters the tale of deliverance was an encouragement
to faith while in others it fell on deaf ears.

On the fifth day of freedom I told Betty. Later I learned
the difficulty it caused; she had received my report in a
confusing ambivalence of alarm and envy that increased her
mounting apprehensions. The alarm concerned my emo-
tional state. Over the past few months my behavior had been
a source of considerable anguish to her, and she knew that if
on principle I was now a non-smoker, the change in my

62

personality was radical enough to warrant close attention. Envy, however, stemmed from quite another source. She was a heavy smoker herself, and several times had tried to break the habit. Then suddenly I was making claim to easy victories in a battle she had lost time and time again, so she found it difficult to rejoice with me. However, her bout with tobacco plays a significant role later in the story. We must set it aside for now, and follow a proper sequence.

It was a short while after the cigarette incident that I awoke one morning at the strange hour of three o'clock. The streets had been empty since midnight and everything was quiet, yet for some reason my mind bustled with activity. Trying to fall asleep proved fruitless, so I went to the kitchen for some hot milk; then after another hour of wakefulness my eyelids grew heavy again and sleep returned. When the same thing happened the next night, a mild concern crept over me. I had always been a sound sleeper; now after only three hours in bed I seemed fully refreshed and, strangely, after another short while the heaviness of sleep returned as quickly as it had left. I was puzzled to say the least.

When for the third consecutive night I awoke bright-eyed and fresh, my memory began reviewing some of the symptoms of depression, and worry set in. So often lately my eyes gave evidence of weeping and although no one knew it, I had been entertaining voices—no, not voices, the voice of God—none the less I was hearing things. Was I becoming insomnolent as well? Spying a Bible among the African violets on a window ledge over the sink, I reached for the Psalms; but the book fell open to Ephesians, and my thoughts lingered there instead. *Had I ever read the first chapter of Ephesians before?* Of course, yes, but there was such an aliveness and immediacy to the message conveyed at that moment, I decided it must be a new translation. A glance at the cover settled the question, and when it proved to be the King James version, I knew that God must be speaking to me in a very special way. *Was it then He who had been waking me these past few nights? Perhaps so—*

startling as the idea was. *But after all, what better time to study than three in the morning, when the doorbell and phone are silent, and the children are asleep?* I read on, and St. Paul's letter assumed such a striking literalness to my mind. For the first time from the Bible, the mystery of the Church in its parochial aspect took on lively dimensions, and my imagination saw the beginning of a new hope. After an hour of devouring the strong meat of those words I was satisfied; sleep came quickly again.

The next night it happened once more—and then the next, and the next. Nightly I was nudged into wakefulness by the finger of God, and a handful of unbroken minutes became solitudes of exhilaration and great excitement. I was reading the Bible as though I had never before read it. Daily led by the Spirit—often in mental impressions of chapter and verse—I was introduced to the possibility of Christ's *fullness* being revealed in a local manifestation of His body. It was to a little congregation in Ephesus that St. Paul revealed his prayer, "that you may be filled with all the fullness of God." The loftiness of St. Paul's claims for the local congregation astonished me; his words began searing in my memory a picture of unimaginable integrity between the risen Christ and a parish church. Yes, a parish church! I began to see visions of lay commitment to ministry, and of corporate life in the Christian community such as few high-churchmen have dared to look at. There were visions of real, creative power: the organism of God's people in love and in faith, openly sharing the fullness of their entire lives with each other; a power to become Christ Himself—another enflesh-ment, not in arrogant, self-important ways which would be the fruit of a mere human endeavor but in a paschal sense— the same Christ available in the world today, still doing the works of compassion done once in His own flesh by the power of the Spirit. I suppose an amazing aspect of this beginning of visions was concreteness and practicality. They were as specific (though initially vague) as an architect's model; and perceiving them not as a theological exercise but as a guidepost to an immediate expression of Christ's life in Houston's East End, I had a glimpse of the new Redeemer Church. Everything within me thrilled at the sight!

For several weeks I must have appeared dazed. They were marvelous weeks of intensive concentration in the world of Scripture, an experience somehow missed in seminary. Oh yes, I had taken courses in the Bible and had done well; but now the word of God had me enchanted! As it was with David of Israel, it had become a delight to my soul, and each morning my mind was renewed by it as I awakened eager to hear what God was going to say that day. There had developed a prophetic ring to scripture that was exciting. The word of God always had a place of importance to me, especially in preaching, but now it was taking on a whole new significance; God Himself was speaking to my innermost being, and listening to His words, how could I doubt the vision imparted through His own lips?

Weeks became months and I grew confident of the voice that was speaking during those nightly trysts. There was not a single doubt that it was the voice of God. However, no sounds were heard; no impressions were received, no feeling stimulated from the environment of creatures around me. No. Properly speaking it was not a voice that sounded any more than there were words I was listening to. It was the Person of God my spirit heard, Spirit to spirit, a still small voice behind the wind and thunder, and behind the words of the Bible too. I knew the thoughts I was identifying as God's voice were experienced in the same way as were all my thoughts; the feelings, desires, and imaginings were my own. I knew also, however, that God was using these familiar means to communicate with me. It was in the terms of my own humanity He was revealing His mind to the condition of my life, and I was learning a new level of trust in Him and in myself. A most important discovery was unfolding before me: simple acceptance of oneself is the ground on which the Sons of the living God walk peacefully with their Father and at liberty with one another.

The family spent August of 1964 in North Carolina vacationing at the home of Betty's parents. Before we left Houston I gave serious consideration to dropping the family off and going on to New York—perhaps that would be my only chance to visit Dave Wilkerson and see his work in Brooklyn—but since funds for the family vacation were already thinly stretched I set the idea aside for later. However, it soon became apparent the Lord had a different plan.

A day or so after we settled in at North Carolina I awoke at an even earlier morning hour than usual; my thoughts were scattered, and rather than attempt some Bible reading I set the book aside and prayed. The core of my being was strangely agitated. One of the side benefits of early morning devotions had been the discovery that at times of distraction I could command my soul to be still—to bless Him with praises, in effect—and then when at peace, my ears became more attuned to the sound of His voice. That morning while I gave thanks for such a gift of confidence to hear Him, He spoke. *Go to New York,* He said clearly. I asked, *When?* and He replied, *Next Tuesday.* Hesitating I wondered about the matter of finances, and then was gladdened by a gentle reminder, *I can be trusted for that. Do as I say.* So later in the morning I called New York and ascertained that Dave Wilkerson would be in his office the following Thursday, and I resolved to meet him there sometime that day.

Of course Betty overheard the call and when I turned from the telephone in the hallway, seeing her in the next room looking at me quizzically, I thought, *Bless her heart. I wish I could be reassuring and tell her everything's alright. There's that fear in her eyes again . . . But we don't seem to able to talk these days.* Her response to my plan was condescending.

"Graham, where do you intend to get the money for the trip?" she inquired distantly.

"Well . . ." I hesitated, "I know you'll think it's funny when I say it, Betty, but I'm going to anyway. The Lord will look after that for me."

"How?" was her flat response.

I decided to uncover the whole thing: "I don't know ... but He told me this morning in my prayer time I could trust Him for it. I'll take the five dollars I've got in my pocket and the Gulf card for gasoline, and that's it," I said emphatically.

She cast her eyes heavenward in dismay but there was no argument.

Months later Betty confessed that when she realized I was serious about going to New York her confidence in our life together in Houston faltered; she decided to stay in North Carolina, knowing the children would be safe there from my growing instability. However, her mother saved the day when Betty brought the issues to her for counsel. "Betty," she said, "I want you to consider two things. First, Graham's the Lord's anointed, my dear, don't touch him; and remember he's your husband, you need to do as he says."

The next Monday night was the eve of my departure and sleep was slow in coming, so around two o'clock I slipped silently from the bedroom and went to the front study. It had been a warm night and the windows were raised, but by now there was a cool, moist breeze. Sitting quietly for a long time I listened to the early morning's lisp, and let the darkness soothe me. In time the simple thought, *Romans sixteen,* worked its way into consciousness. I turned on a light, and reaching for my Bible, opened it in the New Testament and read. *Something's odd,* I thought, *not much nourishment here. Maybe I heard wrong.* But I persisted, and working through the long list of greetings and exhortations brought me at length to the twenty-fifth verse where Paul's words stood out boldly.

> Now to him who is able to strengthen you according to my gospel and the preaching of Jesus Christ, according to the revelation of the mystery which was kept secret for long ages but is now disclosed and through the prophetic writings is made known to all nations, according to the command of the eternal God, to bring about the obedience of faith—

The gospel in the prophets? It had not occurred to me the gospel of Paul and the preaching of Jesus were matrixed in the prophets of old. *No wonder my reading's been limited to the New Testament,* I marvelled. *God would've had a difficult time getting me to believe I could find the gospel in the old.* Diffidently turning to a place closer to the middle of the Book, I opened at the second chapter of Joel, and recognizing it, embarked on the familiar theme for Ash Wednesday. *Was this powerful call to repentance meant for me?* I was quickly entwined in its message and when the twelfth verse came along, my comprehension was struck so deep that it caught my breath.

> "Yet even now," says the Lord, "return to me with all your heart, with fasting, with weeping, and with mourning"
>
> (Joel 2:12)

Fasting ... weeping ... mourning, I mused. *Do you suppose the Lord wants me to go to New York fasting? That's one way to save money, but I've never done that sort of thing before. Okay,* I ventured, *I'll do it and see what happens.*

Betty exchanged an uneasy farewell with me later that morning, and I left. Traveling while fasting was pleasant—it was not a total fast, there being the occasional glass of juice or cup of tea—and I arrived at my destination the following Thursday morning refreshed. Brooklyn's streets, in the environs of Teen Challenge Center, reminded me of Houston's East End: old homes, some of them abandoned, and unkempt property everywhere. While parking the car I became excited. *What will we say to each other?* I thought, *I wish I'd read his book—that'd be a good opener.* Entering the building where Dave Wilkerson was to be found I approached the receptionist. She took my name and offered me a chair in the crowded waiting room. I asked her when he would see me. "Oh, there's no way to tell," she said cheerfully. "He'll see you sometime today, but these people are ahead of you." A

68

sweep of her hand encompassed almost two dozen souls—many of them disheveled and pitiable—who were waiting to see the popular Assembly of God minister. Disappointment surged as suddenly as excitement had, and hiding my anger behind a proud facade I said, "Ask him if he'll see me tomorrow by appointment." The friendly woman stepped behind a closed door and in a few moments came back to report, "Tomorrow afternoon at four." I thanked her and left the building.

Before reaching the car I realized an embarrassing fact: *Graham, you have no money! And you don't know anyone in New York. Where are you going?* The Vales had told me they stayed at the Center while they were in Brooklyn, and that had been my plan, too, until that obvious display of my self-importance interfered. Looking at the Center across the street I thought, *I can't go back in there now, I just can't do it.* When seated in the car I bowed over the steering wheel and prayed, *Lord, that was sheer pride, please forgive me. What do you want me to do? Go to Trinity Church in Manhattan*, He said, and there was an added word, *Then find Lillian Corner.*

Manhattan's Broadway at Wall Street is a long drive from the Teen Challenge Center in Brooklyn, and it was well past noon before my car was nestled in a parking space not far from Trinity Church. There were several visitors inside wandering up and down the aisles of the nave, pausing to read plaques and inscriptions. They were chatting quietly among themselves. Refusing a proferred tourist leaflet I entered the church and went directly to the choir area which had been closed off with a braided silk cord barrier and a sign, "Visitors Please Keep Out." *Would I be regarded as a visitor?* I wondered. There was a hidden place behind the organ bench and finding it I knelt to pray. Soon a gentle weeping began; there was no paroxysm of pain or facial contortion, but tears rolled in profusion down my cheeks while in grief I prayed for the parish back home, fervently asking that it be given an honest life and ministry.

A young man in working clothes approached my covert about an hour later; his face looked angry and he demanded, "What are you doing here?" "I'm praying," was my simple reply. "Well get the hell out, can't ya read?" he snarled, pointing to the pendant sign. The man was young—no more than eighteen—perhaps a summer supply sexton, so I said nothing but quickly stepped over the cord and returned to the street.

Once in my car again I puzzled about what could be done with the name, Lillian Corner, in New York City; there was no doubt in my mind the Lord told me to find her. Lillian was an intimate friend who lived in Austin. She was a rough-hewn Texas gem, one of the most personable women I had ever met. We became fast friends in seminary days and during the early years of our marriage Betty and I felt as much at home with the Corners as with our own parents who were many miles away. *Sure would like a piece of her angel food cake,* I thought suddenly, catching myself in the midst of a smile. Lillian was a superb cook, of everything, really, but the most delicate of angel food cakes lathered in mounds of boiled icing was her *piece de resistance.* Perfection in home cooking and the name Lillian Corner were to me almost synonyms. In recent years on my mid-September birthday she and her husband arrived faithfully at the Pulkingham residence (wherever it happened to be that year) bearing one of her cakes; and the whole family enjoyed an evening with "Granny Corner" and "Uncle Dick."

There was only one clue that my memory offered the present situation: Lillian had a brother—his name escaped me—whose family I had met once in Austin. Remembering that his home was in Lincoln Park, New Jersey, there seemed only one thing to do. I located it on a map and decided to drive the fifty miles from Manhattan in search of him. Lincoln Park was a small town, a crossroads really, and there was no difficulty in describing the family to a woman I chanced upon; fortunately she was their personal friend and gave exact directions to the Gillette farm a mile outside of

70

town. *Gillette!* That was Lillian's maiden name and my memory was stirred the moment the woman said it. Following her directions brought me quickly to a sinuous driveway where I was to turn left. As I approached the farm house a figure appeared at the front door. *Could it be? It was. Lillian!* She was visitng her brother. In a boisterous embrace we rejoiced at seeing each other and in short order I had been provided with a comfortable bed and a bountiful board for the length of my stay in New York.

We spent the evening together, Lillian and I, reminiscing and swapping home-spun gossip, but my current adventures were only lightly touched upon because I was fearful of receiving a response from her that was similar to Betty's. In the course of conversation cooking was mentioned and when talk of her cakes brought to mind my approaching birthday Lillian said, "Listen friend, I'm going to be teaching this year in September, and you're down in Houston so I can't bring a cake to you on your birthday. Sorry about that." She reached in her purse and produced some bills. "Here," she said, "it's an early birthday present, enjoy yourself." There was enough money in my hand to cover outstanding costs of the New York trip. I was astounded at God's ways.

Dave Wilkerson spent an hour with me the next afternoon. I was unusually free in his presence and we talked of problems and other matters related to ministry, and we talked of some personal things, too. He was a wiry fellow, extremely intense and it struck me as odd that he should be constantly muttering praises under his breath, "to encourage myself," he commented. (I had begged his pardon once, forcing him to explain his mutterings.) We prayed together and he invited me to join him in some street work the next night. Then he said, "I think the Lord has something more for you than just going on the streets with me. I'm going up-state Sunday afternoon and coming back Monday, will you go with me?" "Yes," I returned immediately, trying to cover my surprise at his generosity to a complete stranger. We parted, and my car was soon mingling with the flow of rush hour traffic to New Jersey.

The next day was a hot Saturday in mid-August so I stayed on the farm and rested, but left early enough to spend suppertime in Trinity Church praying. I had decided to break the fast after the street work that night because it was so difficult to find graceful excuses from the Gillette table. Strangely, I still felt drawn to the Church's forbidden organ bench area and chancing another abrupt intrusion returned there. Once again I wept and from among the tears emerged a recognition that God was bringing about in me what He had commanded in the second chapter of Joel. "Turn to me," He had said, "with fasting, and with weeping, and with mourning." Fasting had felt comfortable for the past five days; and there were copious tears. What does the mourning mean? I asked the Lord, timorously.

After the corn falls in the ground and dies, it bears much fruit, He said, but first it must die. You want to see a whole new ministry and a whole new church and so you will; but first you must be a dead man released from every shred of self-interest and from whatever remains of the traditional image you have of your ministry, your personal life, and the church. You must be free from caring what you do, or how you do it, or where, or when—except as it pleases me.

Lord, I don't know what kind of ministry or church it will be, I answered, *but I know the kind I've experienced so far isn't any good. It's useless. Show me the way—I don't care what the consequences are. Please show me a new way.*

Remaining quietly on my knees I allowed random thoughts to mingle indiscriminately with prayers; while meditating, my mind was vibrant with a sense of wonder and expectation beholding the manner of God's leading and care. Some time later (it was dusk) my feet had no more than touched the Broadway pavement when God spoke.

Kneel down.

I turned to re-enter the church in search of a pew.

No, out here on the street. He said.

My soul filled with horror and for three quarters of an hour I ambled from corner to corner, chagrined. On a late Saturday afternoon in summer there are not crowds of people in downtown Manhattan, only a few stragglers and tourists, but my pride vaunted its power none the less. It occurred to me I could throw coins on the street and kneel to retrieve them, certain that no one would criticize a man for stooping to rescue his wealth, but the prospect of kneeling simply at God's command—without obvious excuse—was humiliating, and my knees were like cast iron.

How appalling, I thought. *Can fervent vows be so lightly made? Or, are you going to tell yourself, Graham, that God didn't speak that word to you? If not, then how do you know He ever did speak to you? Listen, Graham, you promised— no one here knows you, what difference does it make?*

Don't make a fool of yourself, pride bantered. *They'll carry you away in a strait jacket.*

Finally, in humility (or was it humiliation?) I knelt at a front corner of the church facing a grave yard. Admittedly, it was done surreptitiously—I looked nowhere but down—but I knelt; and something of my pride withered.

That night a group from Teen Challenge left the Brooklyn Center in a van at ten o'clock and drove to Harlem. When we reached the area, teams of workers dispersed in the crowds; joining Dave Wilkerson and two others I started out, walking uneasily down the middle of teeming, refuse-laden avenues. Intermittently I wept. Nothing in particular stimulated tears, but the complex of evil and suffering that had trapped so many miserable thousands overcast my spirit with a shroud of hideous oppression. Everywhere pushers, prostitutes, and panders from the age of eight to eighty were wandering the streets at two in the morning among crowds I was accustomed to seeing only at mid-day; even babies in make-shift cribs squalled unnoticed by the curb while their parents hovered in clusters at shadowy doorstoops.

When we passed through a particularly dense mob moving down a dark side street, Dave enquired whether I would like to see a "shooting gallery." Having no idea what he meant I said without feeling, "Yes." It turned out to be a walking nightmare. Down under the streets in myriad conduit tunnels that join tenement to tenement at the foundation, we crept from one foul crypt to another. Passing through human excrement and over lousy lust-stained mattresses, our path led eventually to an isolated corner where a half dozen boys were main-lining drugs. They were taking their doses in amounts small enought to sustain a lingering euphoria; one had a needle poised at an ankle when we entered—his arm veins were collapsed, I was told. They were like six strangers sharing a grotesque *danse macabre;* panting, witching, and muttering incoherently to the shuffle of an unsung dirge. We watched unnoticed for fully fifteen minutes.

Shooting gallery, I thought. *It's a demonic prayer meeting! My God, look at those pathetic creatures. They're possessed!*

Our return to the street was by way of a jagged hole under the brick staircase of an abandoned tenement house; emerging into the night I looked across the way and saw a large sign advertising the work of one of the major Christian denominations. Under the sign was a smaller one, "Saturday Nite Social 9-12 Dancing, and Refreshments," it read. The empty building was pitch black and the doors were locked; in the streets the devil was having his fling. A wave of nausea gripped me and flooded my mind with despair for the church's fraudulence. Everywhere the intensity of misery was crass and relentless. I was finally forced to withdraw in a state of semi-shock; being unable to bear the pain of participating any longer in those broken lives, I became an observer and wept.

The next day Dave welcomed me at his Staten Island home and we left from there to drive up-state. The night was passed in an old tourist hotel in the Adirondacks after a pleasant day filled with the testimony of a man remarkably used by God. His muttered praises no longer struck me as odd. When the business at hand was accomplished early the next morning, we headed south, stopping in Poughkeepsie at an old estate about an hour north of the city. There was a new work beginning there; the mansion was to be converted into a home for women rescued from the city streets, and Dave wanted to confer with the man he had placed in charge.

It was there I received the baptism with the Spirit.

I can scarcely remember the room it happened in now. In retrospect it seems it was very large, a library, or perhaps a study serving as an office; we had really just got settled after a two-hour trek. Upon arriving at the estate in mid-afternoon, the three of us—Dave, the man in charge, and I—had traipsed across graceful hills descending to the banks of the Hudson; presumably the others were making some sort of inspection tour and I tagged along at the rear, enjoying the scenery. Once back in the mansion, dinner was announced for five-thirty, and while we waited my two companions chatted quietly at one end of the office; at the other end I stood browsing by a book shelf. Without explanation Dave turned to me and announced, "I bear witness on my heart about you."

What does he mean by that? I wondered.

My doubts were short lived. "Kneel down," he said, "I want to pray."

I knelt and they came across the room hurriedly. When their hands touched my head something inside of me leapt with gladness and even the unusual manner of their prayer was not offensive—it was loudly proclaimed in languages that were entirely foreign to me.

I recall a fleeting thought. *That's unknown tongues, it sounds strange.* But it was alright, and I settled down.

Exactly when the transition happened has faded from memory, but rather soon after I knelt, all awareness of the men and their prayers, of the room, and even of myself was obliterated by the immense presence of God's power. He was unmistakably there, and my inner response was like the clatter of a bamboo wind chime in a gale; the very foundations of my soul shook violently.

75

My God, I thought, wonder-struck, *What's going on?*

A nascent idea dawned then, and as it slowly matured into consciousness my soul gasped and held its breath. *Those prayers for a powerful ministry are being answered! Right now! Great God, can it be?*

In a moment of breathless adoration all my longing for love was satisfied and my inner being was swept clean of defilement from the tip of my toes to the top of my head as with a mighty rush of wind.

" 'What is man that thou art mindful of him, and the son of man that thou visitest him,' " I stammered; and before the last words were formed I had bowed my head to the ground and still kneeling, wept convulsively. The contrast between the magnitude of God and my pettiness had undone me.

"We can go now, the Baptizer's here," said Dave to his companion, and they departed.

Presently the weeping stopped, and I rose to my feet with a sense of strange buoyancy. The Baptizer had done His work, and I knew that from then on my ministry would be one of Godly power. *If there were wings to carry me to the top of the nearest tree,* I thought, *I'd proclaim the praises of God for miles around.* But I was alone in a very large room so I went in search of company. Shafts of light from the evening sun moved playfully on the walls along my path down a long hallway to the dining room; their color was rich and warm, and watching them made me feel at home.

I arrived in time to say the grace at Dave's behest and when it was finished I noticed in the ascription that the Holy Spirit for the first time in my remembrance had a personal place in the Trinity. *Hmm,* I thought, *He's always been an 'it' before. Praise God, He lives—like the Father and the Son!* Supper consisted of boiled new potatoes, fresh green beans, and a meat loaf that was heavily laced with oatmeal. But I think it must have been manna. The portions were meager, and I learnt that our provisions had been bought by scraping together the last pennies of the staff and the handful of girls who were already placed there. The developing

76

work was called by them a faith venture: there was no source of income but what God in His mercy provided. There had been enough money for some meat; the vegetables were an anonymous gift.

The remainder of our trip was very silent. It was dark and I took pleasure in watching a growing aurora of the city lights at the horizon.

I wondered casually what was going to happen to me when I returned to Houston.

Finally Dave spoke. "Y'know, I'm going to tell you something. I've been struggling with it for about half an hour because I'd rather not say it, I guess. I haven't had too much respect for the denominational churches, but I think God wants me to say this to you. Stay in the Episcopal Church. Go back home and submit yourself to your organization and your Bishop, and God will raise up a powerful ministry right where you are. I don't usually tell people that but I think God wants me to say it to you."

I don't suppose he saw my smile in the dark, or heard my silent Praise God, but somehow I think he knew about them anyway.

VI

*Interpreting Spiritual
Truths to those who
Possess the Spirit*
(I Corinthians 2:13)

Our return to Houston was inglorious. I had no illusions that personal theophanies would either be understood or appreciated by disgruntled elements in the parish, but the crisis that confronted me on the morning of our homecoming shoved my New York pilgrimage into the background for a time.

Before leaving on vacation a month earlier, I had secured assistance from nearby clergy in order to supply the parish with a Sunday Eucharist each week, and Father Granville Peaks from the nearest neighboring black flock was scheduled for the fourth Sunday of my absence. The day after his visit the parish treasurer, followed soon by a significant number of parishioners, announced his withdrawal from our fellowship, and as he turned the books over to the senior warden he said, "Years ago I told myself I'd never worship in a church where a black man had preached." Father Peaks' ministry settled an issue that till then had been faced only obliquely—the parish would not again for a very long time harbor champions of the cause of white Anglo-Saxon churchism; the root of Redeemer Church's beginnings, planted during the 1930's in Houston's burgeoning East-End suburb, had now very effectively been cut.

The retiring treasurer, spitefully refusing to sign my

monthly check or one for the amount of Father Peaks' honorarium, gave us no option when he left but to hasten the process of establishing a successor. We made the happy choice of Sam Farquahar whose cheerful optimism proved to be as great an asset as his punctilious bookkeeping. Sam and Lottie had been loyal and useful members of the parish for decades and had served in almost every capacity of leadership open to the lay folk.

Sam was the first evidence of response to what I recognized as a subtle change in my preaching after returning from New York. It was neither the delivery nor the content of the sermons that changed, but rather their preparation and effect. I had always followed the liturgical calendar. However, since the time of being coerced into writing three abstract exercises required for ordination, I had not written a full text (if there was a proper homiletical form, its shape and content entirely escaped me). I had always spoken from a mental outline formulated during hours of drudgery in the study each Saturday. The act of preaching was easy; it was preparation that had been accompanied by an inordinate use of antacids and stomach relaxants until the time my ulcers were healed.

On the first Saturday following our return from vacation I prepared a sermon for the fourteenth Sunday after Trinity. However, the next morning during early service when I turned to the place in the altar book where the Sunday propers had been marked, I saw that my preparations were for the wrong day: it was Trinity Fifteen and I had been away for five, not four Sundays. While I was reciting the collect and epistle, my mind scurried among the various choices available for a course of action. Then some words from the epistle I was reading struck me with unusual force. "For in Christ Jesus neither circumcision availeth anything, nor uncircumcision, but a new creature." When I turned toward the people for the sermon, my mouth opened and I spoke unrehearsed on the subject of new birth. It went well.

The next afternoon about four o'clock came a knock on

my study door. It was Sam looking troubled. "What's the matter Sam?" I asked blithely.

"Oh," he sighed accepting the chair I offered. "I don't know. I was posting some bills and thought I'd come up and say hello."

"Get off early?" I queried.

"No, I can leave when I'm caught up, usually," he said. He was sitting on the edge of the chair inspecting his fingernails. I waited quietly.

"Listen," he said at last, "what you talked about yesterday morning, I never heard it said like that before—I mean about being really born again, really. Do you mean that?"

"Yes," I said simply.

"I don't know whether I'm really a Christian then," he concluded.

"Do you want to be?"

"Sure I do. I've been going to church long enough, I oughta."

"Sam, have you ever talked personally to Jesus and asked Him to come and live His life in you?"

"No, I don't guess so," he answered.

"You want to?"

"Yep."

Sam slipped onto his knees, chin on chest waiting for my lead. We said together a simple prayer of confession and affirmation of faith in the crucified and risen Christ. With the utterance of "Amen," I looked up and saw tears spill from his closed eyelids. In a moment he stood, mopped his cheeks with a handkerchief and said, "Well, that's that. Thank you, parson. See you at the vestry meeting tonight."

"Yes. Praise the living God," I affirmed.

Sam snickered a smile. "A-men," he threw over his shoulder just before closing the door behind himself.

"Praise God," I muttered sitting back in my chair and staring at the ceiling.

That's the first time I've ever seen it happen that way, I thought. *The Lord convicted him of his condition, I didn't . . . did a good job, too! And the Lord led him right here for prayer. And then the Lord touched his heart and obviously met his need.* I mused over God's simplicity and marvelled that an unprepared sermon had stimulated the whole affair.

VII

*And with Great Power Gave
the Apostles Witness of
the Resurrection of the
Lord Jesus: and Great
Grace was upon Them All*
(Acts 4:33)

"The Body of our
Lord Jesus Christ, which was given . . ."

Without altering the tone or pace I listened to my voice
doing a perfunctory task.

"Take and eat this . . .',

The kneeling woman responded with a disarming smile as
I pressed a wafer into her open palm, and my words assumed a new note of personal immediacy. Then I recognized
her as a woman I had met recently across town at a gathering of neo-Pentecostals.

Why, that's Margaret Whyte, I thought. *What in the world
is she doing with crutches?*

". . . in remembrance that Christ died for thee . . ."

Must be her ankle or foot, the way she's kneeling, I speculated, straining to see beyond the heads and shoulders of
bowed worshippers.

". . . and feed on Him in thy heart by faith with thanksgiving."

I was in the act of administering bread to the fourth
person past Margaret when I realized her uncomfortable-
looking posture was still vividly fixed in my mind's eye. The
crutches were beside her resting together on the altar rail,
and with her weight borne by elbows and one knee she had a

81

precarious list. She seemed unperturbed, however. Her eyes were closed and her head slightly thrown back, and there was a warm radiance to her slightly smiling countenance.

When I looked at her face some unsettling questions occurred to me. *Was she not healed by His stripes? And weren't those stripes in His body? Could she find herself healed here in this body while receiving His body?* My mind gave resounding affirmations to each question and I turned toward her before administering bread to the next person. Undoubtedly my actions were observed by everyone approaching the choir and altar rail, and by many who had already returned to their pews, even though I moved and spoke as inconspicuously as possible. Gently laying a hand on Margaret's shoulder I asked the Lord Jesus Christ to extend His mercies toward us at that moment and heal. Without tarrying for an answer I resumed administering the sacrament where I left off.

Some words from the day's gospel came to mind while I was at the altar exchanging paten for chalice.

And Jesus answering spoke unto the lawyers and Pharisees, saying, Is it lawful to heal on the sabbath day? And they held their peace. And he took him, and healed him, and let him go. . .

In a few seconds the words of administration droned on as I passed from person to person.

"Drink this in remembrance that Christ's blood was shed . . ."

One by one the worshippers rose to return to their pews and were replaced by waiting communicants. Glancing to my left I looked and saw the crutches still resting against the rail, but beside them was an empty place. Margaret was gone. I looked down the center aisle and saw her with one foot shod and the other one heavily bandaged and covered with a thick white sock. She was half running, half skipping because of her shoeless gait and I could tell by the animated movements of her head that she must be wreathed in smiles.

The sight of her caused my breath to catch momentarily

healed at L5

and then I ejaculated, half aloud, "Praise God; praise Him for His mercy!" The church was strangely hushed, and a living peace hovered over the congregation for the remainder of the morning's worship. When I turned toward the people at the blessing I had to fight for my composure—I was overwhelmed with a sense of gratitude and awe when my glance fell upon the crutches, alone, resting against the altar rail where Margaret and the ushers had left them.

Afterward in the gymnasium I saw her moving swiftly among the coffee drinkers. An unusual number of people had stayed behind that morning and conversation was brisk and lively. Betty approached me looking stunned and unbelieving. "Did you see what happened to that woman visiting us from across town?" she asked.

"Yes, I did," was my amazed retort, "what was wrong with her foot anyway?"

"It was broken, I heard her tell someone over there," Betty said. "Doesn't she look odd walking around—I mean skipping around—with a shoe in one hand and dragging her crutches in the other? Graham, what in the world is going on here?"

"A spiritual object lesson, I think," I half mused. "Betty, did you notice in the gospel this morning? About the man Jesus healed on the sabbath, I mean? I was very tempted to share with the congregation this morning that I've received some of the gifts of the Spirit, but I felt a warning that if I did I might cause some unnecessary trouble. And, you know, the Lord convinced me ahead of time that He could take care of the testimony of my calling. He called me to preach, and the only thing worth preaching is the cross. He warned me not to preach my personal experiences. Does that make sense to you?"

"Oh, I don't know," Betty said lightly. "I guess it does. But if her getting healed is a part of your sermon it's the best one you ever preached."

"I reckon so," I said laughing. "Well at least this morning's congregation knows there's a gift of healing. I wonder what's going to come of that?"

VIII

*Preaching the Gospel of
the Kingdom and Healing
every Disease and every
Infirmity among
the People*

(Matthew 4:23)

As I heard my voice sounding the concluding sentences to the gospel for the day, there burst into awareness a knowledge that something extraordinary was about to happen. The ascription, "Praise be to thee, O Christ" had been said, and I was filled with an electrifying sense of expectancy; even during the sermon it was difficult to keep from wandering in thought, anticipating what it might be. The words that struck me with such force were from the ninth chapter of St. Matthew:

For whether is easier, to say, Thy sins be forgiven thee; or to say, Arise, and walk? But that ye may know that the Son of man hath power on earth to forgive sins, (then saith he to the sick of the palsy,) Arise, take up thy bed, and go unto thine house. And he arose, and departed to his house. But when the multitudes saw it, they marvelled, and glorified God, which had given such power unto men.

Remembering the recent healing during a Sunday Eucharist, I scrutinized every communicant as he filed to the altar rail, but communion time passed without incident. The service came to a close.

What was that all about anyway? I thought, taking my place at the rear of the procession. *This is heady stuff . . . I need to be careful. Could have sworn that something was going to happen, though.*

While alone and unvesting, I ruminated. *You could really get messed up relying on tangible feelings like that. I remember that funny woman in Austin who claimed that when God wanted her attention he laid a hand on her shoulder in just a certain way. The poor soul was already confused even before she began to 'feel' the hand of God. Sure is a fine line between being led astray and trusting yourself! Yes, and I remember that fella who said that every time he felt an icy grip on his leg he knew God wanted to speak through him. Said it was a sign he was 'under the anointing' ... that's an awful phrase isn't it! Some of that Pentecostal rhetoric really gets me. Then that time I heard him speak! What a hostile god that must have been ... angry and threatening. Phew! Oh well, bless the Lord!*

I passed a few words of conversation with some stragglers from the coffee hour and then went next door to the rectory. Neal Prewitt was there anxiously trying to calm a distraught woman. Before the door was closed behind me the woman grabbed at my arm frantically. "Please, please, where is he?" she begged. With her eyebrows raised, Neal gave me a negative shrug of bewilderment.

"Oh, please, Q.B.'s fallen," the stranger cried with intensity, "I need him."

I had a clue. "Are you looking for M. L. Bush?" I asked.

"Yes," she babbled, "Q.B. fell—she's hurt bad. I can't lift her—she's lying there in the middle of the floor. Where's M.L? Please."

By then I was convinced of the urgency of the situation. "Down in the choir room" I blurted. "You go find him, I'll get over to Q.B."

She hurried away while Neal and I climbed into the car that was parked by the family-room door.

The ignition ground my little Valiant into the sound of a noisy purr beneath the carport, and Neal inquired tentatively, "Is her name Cupie, like C-U-P-I-E?"

"No," I smiled, "it's Q. B., like Q-B. She's Q. B. and he's M. L.—I don't know what, if anything, the initials stand for."

"That woman must be the sister who came to take care of her," I commented as I nosed the car in the direction of the Bush home.

"Has she been sick long?" Neal asked.

"Well, yes. I don't know why she went to the hospital though. But I can understand why she couldn't be lifted; she's really obese—not just too fat, it's dropsy I think. You know, her legs are huge and she uses two canes to walk with. M. L. and Q. B. are old-time members of the parish; he has helped count money after church for years. Good folk!"

"Well, praise God!" said Neal. "I couldn't figure out what she was getting at, she was so excited. Said she didn't go to church here so I thought she must be a neighborhood women who—"

"Here's Clay Street," I interrupted. "It's that white frame one. Y'know, her sister must have run to the church. She really was upset. It's only a few blocks but she's no youngster, is she?"

Since we suspected there was no one to answer a knock we walked in the front door unannounced and headed toward the back of the house. Neal went ahead of me. By the time I had reached the center of the living room there was something welling up from within and I recognized the approach of tears.

That's crazy, I thought. *I don't even know what's wrong with her.*

We passed through the dining room beyond which could be seen a misshapen mass on the linoleum floor. Stepping into the kitchen I caught a closer glimpse at Q.B.'s distorted form. She was lying face up with one leg grotesquely bent and pinned beneath her heavy torso. The unconscious body was hideously twisted, head thrown back and mouth agape. She had the pallor of shock. It was in the flash of a moment that Q.B.'s condition registered on my mind and I thought instantly, something's broken. Then suddenly my breath came in a succession of short sobs—involuntarily—and as at the moment of a sneeze, every nerve in my body loosened and I fell in a heap on the floor. Convulsive weeping came, the way it did when Dave Wilkerson prayed for me in New York. Neal slipped to her knees beside Q.B., placed a hand on her shoulder and began praying rapidly in tongues. In order to prevent the crying from becoming a miserable wail I clenched my teeth so tight, my jaws ached for several days.

Then as quickly as the weeping had begun, it stopped. I looked at the tableau in front of me. Neal had not moved a muscle, she was still praying quietly, her eyes shut. But the body had straightened. Q. B. was flat on her back now, eyes open and looking quizzically at Neal. Then she looked at me and I saw a sparkle of health in her eyes and color in her cheeks. *Hallelujah!* I thought, mopping at my eyes with a soaked handkerchief.

M. L.'s lanky figure appeared from the front of the house and filled the kitchen doorway; his sister-in-law was peering from behind him with a look of utter amazement on her face.

Q. B. spoke. "Help me up," she said.

We raised her to her feet and lent a hand as she walked heavily to a room adjoining the kitchen and climbed into bed.

"Thank heaven she wasn't hurt," said the sister, after we returned to the kitchen. "I was sure she'd broken a leg. Would have been glad to get the glass of water for her, poor dear, but she insisted. Slipped on the linoleum and fell with all her weight right on that leg. How she escaped being hurt I'll never know."

"Maybe she didn't," said M. L. succinctly.

Neal cut her eyes in my direction and gave me a knowing smile. "Praise the Lord!" she said with a lilt to her voice.

"I waved through the door to the adjoining room. "Bye, Q.B." I called. "You alright now?"

"Oh my yes," she said weakly, "thanks to you two. Come back when I'm able to entertain you properly, will you? Thank you ma'am—I don't even know your name," she called to Neal.

"Neal Prewitt. Praise the Lord," said Neal simply, with an engaging smile.

"Yes, yes indeed," said Q.B., a little flustered.

IX

*Grant to Thy Servants
to Speak Thy Word with
all Boldness, while Thou
Stretchest Out Thy Hand
to Heal, and Signs and
Wonders Are Performed
through the Name of
Thy Holy Servant Jesus.*
(Acts 4:29, 30)

Once, when exasperated with excesses in his charismatic prayer group at St. David's Church, Austin, the Rector commented, "Graham, I don't know whether they have something I don't have, or something I don't want."

That was how Betty felt after my baptism with the Spirit. It caused in her a travail of soul which I have seen since in hundreds of solid Christians when faced with Pentecostal gifts. Until my strange experiences in 1964 she had been a secure believer. Her testimony of personal conversion and her commitment to the Christian fellowship had been carefully established before she reached young adulthood in the Methodist Church; now, all at once, the adequacy of her background was being challenged by the drama of my evolving faith. And there were additional complications, too. She had married me because the Lord had told her to, though when she did, it was with a clear look at the vague course my life had taken until then.

We met in 1950 when I was twenty-four and still unsettled. At the University of Western Ontario in my Canadian fatherland, I had wandered aimlessly through a general undergraduate degree involving only a brief flirtation with thoughts of settling in the medical profession. Graduation left me unprepared for the future and I spent three years chasing a musical whim, stopping in the United States where I found a talented wife and a keen taste for living in the land of my birth. At the time of our marriage in September 1951, life had veered along another path: The Episcopal Seminary of the Southwest in Austin had accepted me as a candidate for Holy Orders under the jurisdiction of the Bishop of Texas; finally settling my defection from Canada and from the Roman Catholic communion, I claimed an American birthright.

The beginning years of our marriage were in some respects hectic and not the least of troubles was the loosening of Betty's ties to the Methodist communion, in which she had grown up. She strove valiantly to become a free-thinking Episcopalian, the wife of a liberal-minded cleric. Eventually she did well at it.

So it was that although her struggle following our 1964 vacation seemed to be based in doctrinal opposition to my recent Pentecostal experiences, in reality it was a conflict issuing out of her own anxiety and resentment. I suspect Betty was afraid that if my fresh insights into the Christian faith were valid, her earlier ones were spurious, and she would be forced to abandon the foundations of her religious position, or be found fraudulent. That, I suppose, is reason enough for resentment; but also she was offended at what appeared to be a turn-about action on my part. My fervent new belief was naive and plain, not unlike what she had left behind in her desire to achieve the wifely image she thought would please me. Yet there were enough disturbing differences between the two simple faiths, and a mere return to her former state could not heal the strife. In confusion she tried at first to remain aloof to the situation—common sense required that the changes in me prove stable and permanent before she go running after them for herself—but God would not wait. He was rapidly drawing her with cords of love into a deeper commitment and fellowship.

The pivotal point of Betty's struggle was smoking. That in

itself was humiliating. Her background taught her that if smoking was not a grievous sin, it was at least a despicable practice, and several times during our marriage she had tried to quit. Every attempt failed and with each failure she suffered a defeat of faith. Finally her conscience was salved with the sop that Episcopalians are expected to smoke. Then I broke the habit and she saw that it was done without apparent effort. Her attempts to join me came to nothing. She was desperate about it and remained so for several months. One Friday, when we had been home from vacation for a few weeks, she prayed ardently for a sign of God's ability to deliver from that or any other habit. She was now willing to accept this Pentecostal baptism that her husband so avidly endorsed even though her own understanding had not yet grasped it. The fighting had stopped.

It was during those very same days that I was being enticed by a pernicious sort of heretical spirit. Technically it was a form of gnosticism, I suppose. The effect of that error has been seen in other charismatic ministries, expressing itself in varied ways. The particular form tempting me was associated with the use of physical contact for imparting spiritual gifts. A conviction had crept into my thinking that such behavior was not only useless but redundant. I realize, of course, that this is one of those grey areas of theological understanding where one man's meat is another's poison, and the arguments brought forth in favor of my changing position were superficially sound. *After all, is God not a sovereign power who can manifest Himself any way He wills? Why should He be belittled into conforming to so inadequate a piece of "baggage" as a human being in order to bestow His blessings?* All such questions must be countered with an emphatic statement that He has chosen to manifest Himself in particular ways, and those ways are incarnational. To quote the author of Hebrews, ". . . in these last days he has spoken to us by his Son . . ." So my reluctance to lay hands on the sick for their healing and my aversion to the use of oils or other legitimate "means" as channels of grace were not based upon revelation but resulted from the fancy of some spiritual philosophy.

I have perhaps stated the problem too simply and impersonally; the truth of the matter is that I was in danger of being infatuated with my own spiritual powers. They were very real powers, but they were not mine. My thoughts went something like this: *After all, spiritual things are so much greater in importance than mundane things; this created universe could never do justice to the expression of true spiritual realities. Therefore God is justified in using (or even abusing!) His creation in any whimsical way He wishes just so that it serves the purpose of a spiritual end. Several examples come to mind: God suggested we lay hands on the sick just to get us involved; He doesn't need our hands. Likewise, God could make nonsense out of time sequence in order to produce a miracle.* Although not aware of it at the time, I later recognized that my ministry had been at a critical stage. Had I listened to that seducing voice, I might never have had due respect for the body of Christ which is an essential element in the conduct of a wholesome ministry of the Spirit.

In the middle of the night following Betty's fervent plea for a sign, I roused ever so slightly from a sound sleep and the Lord directed me to lay hands on my wife's quiet form beside me. Drowsily, I did so. Whether (or what) I prayed is lost from memory, and sleep returned at once. Upon awaking in the morning I remarked to myself how strange it was to lay hands on my sleeping wife at the behest of God, when the reason was so hidden from me. Since she made no mention of the matter I concluded that my actions had not disturbed her.

That night, Saturday, Betty and I attended a prayer meeting in the office of a west-end businessman. When the crowd had gathered and we settled into folding chairs arranged in a circle, his wife suggested we bow our heads and wait upon the Lord's leading in prayer. It was our first experience with that particular group of people and I recall thinking that we were involved in something very like a Quaker meeting. When I lowered my head there was a sudden startled gasp to my right. Opening my eyes I cast a glance sideward in Betty's direction and saw her staring at her extended hands. The cause of her surprise was immediately apparent.

Several days earlier she had shown me her hands, where clusters of seed warts were multiplying on the thumb and first two fingers of each. She had been afflicted with them for years, but on two other occasions they had become as extensive as they were now and had required treatment by burning for their removal. When I saw them just a few days earlier, there were dozens in varying sizes, and Betty's comment had been that it was time once again to have them removed. She had gasped because her hands were now totally free of warts.

Instantly I knew when God had removed them, and that simple act disabused my mind of its haughty spirituality. I have never since doubted God's earthly revelation of Himself, both in the life of His incarnate Son and in His historic church.

As for Betty—she had seen God's power. What better sign for a mother than the banishment of a pesky blight from hands that change diapers, wash dishes, comb hair, and tenderly minister in a hundred ways to the children's daily needs. From that time on, when Betty was tempted to smoke she had ready evidence of God's ability to set her free.

The next night we visited a small independent Chinese-American church called Grace Chapel. There among the gentle and self-effacing oriental Christians, Betty received her own baptism of power. It was for me an experience of the most exquisite beauty. Sitting beside Betty was a young girl of about eighteen, and standing nearby were three or four of the Chinese women talking to the pastor's wife, Amy Sit. Most of the congregation had already dispersed, and Betty was waiting her turn for the elder's prayers. Suddenly she stood up, transfigured, with her eyes closed and her hands extended heavenward in a graceful attitude of supplication. Then to my amazement she opened her mouth and began what sounded like an operatic love song in a language I had never heard before. As she did this, the girl beside her arose and, laying one hand gently on Betty's shoulder, began a perfect contrapuntal melody, the two sang a duet in the Spirit. Then the women joined in a chorus in several different tongues, and for perhaps two or three minutes the most angelic sounds I have ever heard filled the small chapel. When the singing stopped there was a breathless hush for a time; we were all standing in various attitudes of prayer drinking in the power of that moment of peace. Finally, Betty broke the silence with a quiet phrase of loving devotion. "Praise the holy name of Jesus," she whispered.

X

He Has Anointed Me to Preach Good News to the Poor. He Has Sent Me to Proclaim Release to the Captives.

(Luke 4:18)

"Operator, he must be at that number, tell them I think he's a prisoner in their jail."

It was nine o'clock Saturday morning and when Betty had taken the message from a Galveston operator two hours earlier she had refused to waken me then. Tommy Browne was calling. He left word for me to call him back because his phone privileges were used up; that probably meant some sort of scrape with the law. When I reached the Galveston number Betty had been given, a male voice answered with a terse "County Court House." Presumably the jail was somewhere near at hand.

"I suppose either one would do, operator, it doesn't matter to me," I said, a little puzzled. She had reported that both Tommy and Manuel Hernandez were trying to reach me; they would locate one and bring him to the phone.

In a moment I heard a pitifully small voice at the other end say, "Hello."

The operator told him his Houston party was on the line; then to me she said, "Go ahead, sir."

"Father?" Tommy interrupted in a stronger voice.

"Yes, Tommy," I said casually, "what's up?"

"Yeh, this is Tommy," he said hurriedly. "Listen, Father, we're in trouble, bad trouble. Can you come down here?"

"What kind of trouble?"

"Oh, I don't know. They think we're murderers or something."

My response to that statement was anything but casual. "Tommy, what are you saying?!"

"Nah, don't get me wrong, Father. We didn't do nothin' like that but, well ... he called it assault and something about murder. Man, we didn't murder anybody though."

"I see. Were you drunk last night?"

"Yeh."

"Cruising the beaches, I suppose?"

"Yeh."

"There must have been more than two of you. The others get away?"

"Yeh."

"What did you do, beat up on someone?"

"Yeh. Bad ... a tire tool."

"Oh my," I moaned. "Was it you or one of the others that did it?"

"It don't matter. I was there, we'll leave it like it is."

"Okay. I'll be there soon. How's Manuel?"

"He's down, man. Listen, Father, we're scared; they're after us and they ain't very friendly down here, neither."

"Alright, I'll be there soon as I can. See you later."

"Okay, Father. Hurry, huh?"

Tommy and Manuel were two of a pack of neighborhood youngsters who had been the bane of my existence since the stormy beginning of a youth program earlier that year. They were all ruffians, about seventeen years old, and drop-outs whose means of support was mostly hidden. However, there was something about these two that appealed to me, especially Tommy. He was unusually gentle at times and on several occasions when we were alone he had used a respectful, "Sir," in the course of conversation.

"This is going to be strange," I thought. "Any other time I've gone to bat for someone, I at least knew their family and background. I don't know anything about these kids except what I've seen . . . or what they've said, and that's not much. Oh well, they're asking for help . . . it's the first time they've done that. I'll see what I can do."

I called a friend, who called a lawyer friend; by ten-thirty we were all on the road to Galveston. As we entered the city, one of them prayed aloud.

"Lord Jesus, you love these kids more than we can imagine. You died to save them from the kind of trap they're in. We're your servants Lord, so lead the way and show us what to do. And, Lord, find a way to show Tommy and Manuel that you love them. We're asking you for a miracle, Lord Jesus." After a few moments of silence there was a chorus of "Amens."

At the door of the court house—a ramshackle, stucco veneer building of great age—we were met by a burly policeman whose response to the name Tommy Browne was vehement.

"Ah, them two!" he exploded. "I'm sure glad we got 'em. Yeh, you can see 'em, come with me."

I exchanged questioning glances with my two friends.

We were led to an office with a sign over its door, "Sam Popovitch, Constable." Mr. Popovitch was in every way a contrast to the policeman who took us to him; he was small in stature, quiet and refined. Since I was wearing a collar he assumed I was the spokesman for the trio.

"What d'you need, Father?" he asked.

"May we see Tommy Browne and Manuel Hernandez?" I requested.

"Sure," he said hesitantly. "You a good friend of theirs?"

"Yes, I've been working with them in Houston for almost a year now. They live near my church."

"They need a good friend." He was a pleasant man—and cautious. After a moment of studying some papers on his desk he looked up and enquired, "One of you a lawyer?"

My companion nodded.

Mr. Popovitch returned to his meditations.

What in the world is he thinking so hard about? I thought.

96

Tommy and Manuel must really be in trouble. Then he looked me full in the face for the first time. "I don't know which they need more, Father, you or a lawyer," he said wearily. "But I'll tell you what: you all go and talk to them and then come back here."

The uniformed man who met us at the front door was waiting in the hall, and at the constable's gesture he led us to two cells, open except for the bars, and unfurnished. Manuel and Tommy were crouching in the back corners of one of them. They were pathetic figures, pale, grimy, and downcast. While the doors were being unlocked they shuffled their way toward us. Tommy had a sheepish grin on his face; Manuel looked angry, and had a large bruise on his left cheekbone. There was not much doubt they were guilty of something.

After I told them we had a lawyer with us, I asked what they wanted me to do.

"Get us out of here," Tommy said. "Look at this place, we've been here all night and there ain't even a chair to sit on."

"Have you had any breakfast?" I enquired.

"Yeh, they gave us donuts and coffee. But I ain't hungry," Tommy said. Manuel grunted; his head was turned about forty-five degrees from me and he had been looking intently at the floor ever since we entered the cell. I later learned it was a characteristic way he controlled his fury.

"What about you, Manuel?"

"Hey, man," he whined without turning his head, "they don't do no more for you than they gotta. I ain't gonna do nothing like this again, I'll tell ya, man."

"Why not?" I was searching for conversation to get his attention.

"I don't wanta spend my life in a hole like this," he said with growing belligerence. "Would you?"

"I guess not," I said. "Well, we'll go and see what we can do about bailing you out or something. I guess there's no use pretending you aren't guilty, is there?"

"Nah, the guy identified us this morning," Tommy said.

"He's up and about then, huh?"

"Yeh, but he's all cut up. We really messed up his face for him. Listen, Father, I ain't gonna drink like that again. I didn't think we'd hurt him as bad as that."

"Never again, Tommy? We'll see," I said with an unbelieving smile.

I called the jailer and we returned to Mr. Popovitch's office.

"What do you think, Father?" the constable asked.

"They're in trouble, aren't they? What can we do to help?"

"Well there's a complication," he said slowly. "You see we've had a lot of muggings like this lately. Mostly Houston punks who come down here to drink on the beach—you know, they're under age so they set themselves up in their car and get plastered. Then they run out of cash. It's dark and lonely down there on the beach, so they jump some unsuspecting soul and frisk him. Trouble with that right now is, a lot of the local folk are up in arms about it. So this bunch of kids last night decide to pick on a medical student who went to the emergency room at the hospital, but he had the sense to call us first and give us their license number. We stopped them just after they got over the causeway, but they scattered in the weeds and we only caught two. Then I got a call from Dr. Otto over at the psychiatry department this morning. He says he wants to give these kids an examination and prove they're criminal types so we can prosecute them fully and make an example out of them."

"Looks bad, huh?" I said sounding resigned. I remembered Dr. Otto from my days as Chaplain at the Galveston medical school, and I knew he meant what he said.

"Yes, but I don't know. There's something about that Browne kid. The Mexican's pretty mean, though. You say you've been working with them?"

"Yes, not a great deal, but they keep coming around the church. I wish I could help them more."

Mr. Popovitch studied the ceiling for a few seconds. I could tell he was counting the cost of something. Finally he said, "Suppose I release them to your custody, do you think they'll do what you say? Can you take some time with them?"

"Yes, on both counts." His suggestion stunned me.

"You'll have to bring them down here for Dr. Otto's examination, and then again when they go before the judge. You sure you won't have any trouble?"

"Pretty sure," I said, hoping my apprehensions were well hidden.

He called to the burly man in the hall, "Bring those two in here, will you, Bert." Then he rummaged through some papers on his desk, found the one he was looking for and jotted my name, address and telephone number at the bottom of it. "I'll keep a record of all this," he said, "but I won't process their cases until later. Come and see me when I notify you about Dr. Otto's examination and we'll talk some more. Thanks Father . . . gentlemen," he said, rising. "They'll bring them to you in the hall. You'll be hearing from me."

This guy has a lot of authority, I thought. *I'm glad he's got a big heart to go with it.*

When Tommy and Manuel were ushered into our presence, they looked around to see where they were being taken. I nodded my head toward the front exit and they stared at me, unbelieving. "Come on," I said, "we're going back to Houston."

"Man, we're free," Tommy chortled, hurrying toward the doorway and running into the street. Manuel was close behind.

While driving out of town we told them what had happened; both vowed absolute obedience to my every whim and with adolescent mirth promised to change their ways immediately.

As we left the causeway and headed north past Texas City, I began to weep. It was the same sort of weeping I had done in Trinity Church, Manhattan—quiet, deep, and with a profusion of tears.

Tommy and Manuel were with me in the back seat. I was

in the middle. Their mirth subsided into an embarrassed silence when they noticed my weeping, but I was disinclined to check it, and without emotion I wept the rest of the way home. When we arrived at the church neighborhood, I got out at the chapel door; Tommy and Manuel professing weariness, wanted to be taken home.

The chapel was empty, and kneeling in a back corner I wept and prayed for the maimed student and Dr. Otto, for the constable and the burly cop, for Tommy and Manuel, and for the kids who got away.

They're really helpless, I thought. *Lord, can't you do something with their lives?*

I sat back exhausted and rested my head against the wall. In a moment the upstairs chapel door scraped against its metal frame and I heard stealthy footsteps on the stairway. Tommy tiptoed in, and knelt beside me; I slipped to my knees.

"Father," Tommy began soulfully, "how come I always do bad things? I don't wanta do wrong, but I can't seem to help it."

"Tommy," I said, putting my hand on his shoulder, "when there's something good inside you, then you'll start doing good things. It's like this: everyone of us is run around by the devil because he's got a claim on our souls until we ask Jesus to come and live inside us to make us His property. When you quit griping about the bad that happens to you, and quit trying to prove to yourself you had a right to do it or that somebody pushed you into it, then you can call it sin. And Tommy, until Jesus owns you, you're so full of sin that you are sin. But you know, Tommy, He really loves you. He died for your sin. You've done the sinning, He did the dying for it; and Tommy, when you turn to Jesus and confess you're a sinner, He'll take your sin and it'll die on His cross with Him. He'll take it away. Then when you ask Him to, He'll come to you and take the place of sin. He'll live in you, Tommy. Then there'll be somebody good inside you and good things can start happening."

While I was speaking he stared dead ahead at the sanctuary lamp. Without turning he suddenly spoke tenderly, "Jesus, I am a sinner like he says, you know that, but I don't wanta be that way anymore. Please come and take it—and you live in me. Please?" There were tear stains on his grimy cheeks. I lowered my forehead to his shoulder where my hand had been and whispered, "Praise God." Tommy's body relaxed and cradling his head in his arms on the pewback in front of us, he wept openly. I had never seen any of the neighborhood kids broken before.

Tommy had been gone for only five or ten minutes when I heard the door upstairs open again. Footsteps descended the stairway. It was Manuel. He asked the same question and I gave the same answer; but he had a hardness that was absent from Tommy and he seemed unable to volunteer himself in prayer.

I said, "Manuel, don't you want to confess that you're a sinner, and ask Jesus to take up His life in you?"

"I tried but nothin' would come out," he said through clenched jaws, battling with emotion.

Putting my hand on his shoulder I prayed softly, "In the name of Jesus be loosed. I command this dumb spirit to loose him, at once!"

Instantly Manuel blurted in a loud voice, as though the sound must travel a great distance upward or not be heard, "God?" He seemed somehow assured of an audience because he continued in a quieter voice, "You know all about me and I'm a sinner. If you can forgive me, send Jesus to live in my heart. I sure hope I ain't gone too far for you to save me." He fell to a silent study of the filigree sanctuary lamp, and then concluded, "Thank you, God."

I smiled a little in spite of myself. Manuel was not weeping; in fact his face was expressionless, but the sound of his voice was genuine.

I was not inclined to probe too deeply into the boys' activities after that; the Galveston incident had terrified them and not until the court proceedings were past would they be able to draw an easy breath. That had some advantages with respect to motivation for self control, but I recognized the disadvantages, too: a conversion born out of fear of punishment lives only so long as unresolved guilt encourages it. *When the guilt goes, I reasoned, and they still control themselves, then the conversion is probably more than skin deep.*

We had opportunity to deal with that matter regularly. Tommy and Manuel, always together, managed to appear unannounced at the rectory or parish building several times each day. Under the guise of seeking current information about their court affair, they reached out to me for reassurance in the only way they knew. There was a lot of jesting and sometimes scoffing, but the message was getting through: they had given Jesus their sin; He had taken their lives in His hands, and nothing would happen that He was not in control of. And further, they could trust Him because more than anything else He loved them and wanted to take care of them. This truth was repeated day after day, and in as many ways as my imagination afforded; they were beginning to hear with the inner ears of the spirit, and I could see the guilt dissolving slowly.

In a few weeks I received a message from Mr. Popovitch. Dr. Otto's examination of the two boys had been set for ten o'clock the next Tuesday and would be followed immediately by their appearance before the court of Judge Gustafsen.

We arrived at the court house in an air of excitement; Tommy and Manuel were flushed with anxiety.

"Hey, Father," Tommy said nervously, "what's that head doctor gonna do?"

"Just ask you some questions, Tommy," I answered off-handedly, "you know, he's going to try and find out if your bad all the way through or not."

"How can he do that?" Manuel queried, wide-eyed.

"Oh ... all he can do is make an opinion, Manuel. But

listen, the Lord's got you safe, you're not all bad . . . Jesus is in you. Dr. Otto will see that."

"Man, I hope so," Manuel said earnestly.

A woman appeared at the waiting room door and said, "Father Pulkingham?" I smiled at her and she continued, "Dr. Otto would like to speak to you, will you come with me, please."

The last time Dr. Otto and I had conversed with each other almost five years earlier, he had raised serious questions about the practice of calling on psychiatric patients whose doctor had not specifically ordered a chaplain's visit. It was a mild and polite altercation, but I felt it was on an important issue, namely, whether the power of prayer is obstructed by the confused mind of a believer. If so, then obviously only the doctor can determine when, if ever, the patient is ready for prayer, which should be administered under his direction in the same manner as any other comforting balm. If, however, prayer could effect a change in the confused state of mind, then it might well be solicited in certain cases as a tool of fundamental importance in the healing process. Dr. Otto was unsympathetic to the latter point of view.

I was ushered into a small consultation room and when the doctor rose to greet me I could tell by the expression on his face that his opinions had not changed significantly.

"How did you get involved in this?" he asked after a few initial formalities.

"These kids are from the neighborhood of my parish in Houston," I answered. "They've been sort of hanging around the church for about a year now."

"Think you've done them any good?" he asked honestly.

"Not until recently," I said, with the same honesty.

"What do you mean?" he probed.

"Well, one of the results of this difficulty they're in is that they've been really converted to Christ." I felt the uneasiness in my voice when I said those words, knowing what his response would probably be.

103

"Oh, you think so, do you?" he challenged dryly. "Well, whatever happened isn't going to change their characters, and I intend to find out if they're criminal types like I think they are. If so, the least we can do is keep them from running loose in society ... for everybody's protection, including theirs."

"Well, I'm confident you'll find that won't be necessary," I concluded, "I see a genuine repentance in them."

"Maybe," he said as he beckoned to the woman to bring one of the boys in.

I passed Tommy in the hall as he was approaching the consultation room; he looked at me with pleading eyes. "Everything's okay, fella," I said smiling.

Back in the waiting room I could see that Manuel's face was tight with emotion. He usually fought down fear with anger and I wondered how he would handle the present situation where anger could only cause him trouble, and he knew it. I thought it wise not to engage him in conversation.

By eleven o'clock we were all in the busy courtroom. Dr. Otto gave a slip of paper to Mr. Popovitch who passed it to a clerk standing next to the bench. She pressed it in her hand with several other papers and nodded to a uniformed officer at the other end of the bench. He consulted a book and then called in a loud voice, "Tommy Browne and Manuel Hernandez, please come forward." The two boys marched, almost military-like, to a position in front of the judge. He stared at their rigid forms for a second, and then glanced at the papers the clerk had handed him. Looking up, he searched the courtroom and when his eyes fell on me he asked, "Are you a friend of these two?" Standing up I nodded assent. "Will you approach the bench, please," he said.

The judge motioned me to come close so Tommy and Manuel were unable to overhear our conversation.

"On Mr. Popovitch's recommendation," he confided, "I am going to put Browne and Hernandez in your custody instead of handing them over to the grand jury. The psychia-

104

trist seems to think they will be in trouble very soon again no matter what we do, but Mr. Popovitch is assured you can handle the two. I intend to read aloud the charge against them and ask what they plead—I'm told it will be 'guilty'—then I will put them in your charge with the warning that if at any time during one year from today you find it necessary to report them to this court, I will prosecute them on the charges here preferred. Is that agreeable to you, sir?"

"It is indeed," I replied.

When the judge told Tommy and Manuel they were in my custody their shoulders straightened, their heads lifted and they smiled visibly. Dr. Otto rose to leave, and I hurried to intercept him and say good-bye.

"I'm glad you weren't too hard on them," I said smiling.

"I was honest," he replied. "There seems to be some remorse in them, some signs of conscience and grasp of right and wrong; but they're disturbed kids who aren't to be trusted, and I suppose I could feel sorry, too, if I had a charge over my head like they've had. Seems to me it wouldn't do any harm at all to salt them away for a year or two and help their conscience out a bit."

"I don't think they're going to need that Dr. Otto," I interrupted, laughing.

"I'll tell you what," he said. "I'll give you $100.00 for each one of them if he hasn't had another scrape with the law at the end of this year under your custody."

"It's a deal," I agreed, shaking his hand.

"It's a bet," he retorted, "and a sure one for me at that."

A short time later, Tommy recieved the baptism of the Spirit and began to recognize his need for a stabler life. He joined the Marines; and passing successfully through boot camp, he went to his first assignment to duty and, as far as I know, to a stable life.

The real test of Manuel's conversion came less than a month after his appearance in court. He was an infamous fighter among the East-end Latin Americans, and was feared as a kicker; that is, his Texas boots and his oxfords had long, hard pointed toes and were used as vicious weapons of offense by somehow affixing a razor blade in the tip of each of them. Several Mexican toughs were after his blood because of the damage Manuel had inflicted on them or their friends.

One night quite late when he and Tommy were walking home from the rectory they recognized the car of Manuel's worst enemy approaching from the rear. They broke into a run and cut through a service station driveway for the safety of back alleys. It was too late. There was a screech of tires and the car lurched in front of them forcing Manuel—who was bringing up the rear—to stop in his tracks. Tommy escaped at a gallop while six hefty Latins wielding chains and switch-blades poured from the car and moved menacingly toward their quarry. Tommy watched from a distance. The bright lights of the car shone blindingly in Manuel's face so his head was slightly turned with that characteristic downward glance; his arms were spread-eagle and his entire body, hands palm-down, was flattened against the garage door. Standing absolutely motionless while his jeering foes accosted him, Manuel muttered over and over again, "Jesus don't want me to fight. Jesus don't want me to fight. Jesus don't want me to fight." The swinging chains were only inches away from Manuel's face when suddenly, before a blow was struck, the six thugs withdrew into their car and drove away.

The next morning after Tommy related the incident to me I asked Manuel his thoughts about what happened the night before.

"Man, that God stuff's strong, ain't it?" he said almost reverently, shaking his head in wonder.

One day early in 1966 I wrote to Dr. Otto, reminding him of our wager and reporting a clean slate for both Tommy and Manuel. He sent me a check for $200.00 with a note expressing his gratitude to me for helping them.

XI

*For the Promise Is to
You and to Your Children
and to all that Are Far
Off, every One whom the
Lord Our God Calls
to Him.*

(Acts 2:39)

A man once compli-
mented his wife by saying that he could not recall life before
marriage.

By the end of 1964 I could scarcely remember ministry
before my charismatic experience of the Holy Spirit. Every
day for four months had been so busy with the astonishment
of miracles that time slowed to an everlasting and heady
gait. Finally 1965 lumbered in. I suppose because with each
wonder there went a noise of fame abroad, it became wide-
spread knowledge along Texas' Gulf Coast that I was a
tongues-speaker. I, or rather my ministry, was becoming
notorious in some circles. Those were days before pentecostalism was a fashionable new movement. Average Episcopalians understood the phrase "tongues-speaker" to mean a
great deal more than just a blabbermouth; the most kindly
connotation offered was cultural puerility in the way of holy
rollers, or perhaps a mindless sort of biblicism.

Oh, but there was a great deal more than that! In the mind
of his accuser, the symptoms of the enthusiast's plight are
many. There is the cloying, non-liturgical, "Praise the Lord,"
or, "Hallelujah!" There is going to meetings at the drop of a
hat, and endless repetitions of ridiculous choruses, and
hand-clapping in church! There is too much talking of the

107

blood of Jesus, too many magical ejaculations of His name—and all that snarling at the devil too. There is disrespect for authority, irresponsibility toward linear commitment, over-emotionalism in worship, and the sanctification of private opinions by the use of proof-texts. There is independence and self-assertion, arrogance and self-righteousness. And then there are the paranoid barriers of hardened doctrine behind which little groups gather protectively.

Indeed, by 1965 those who had heard rumors of my experience in New York suspected I was no longer an Episcopalians' kind of man.

I might well have been some unfortunate pariah or an Ishmael in public gatherings: there were some people who skirted my presence; in private confrontation their discomfort was obvious. At a diocesan conference during those days a classmate from seminary encountered me head-on in a narrow hallway. Recognizing who he was approaching, he was taken aback and his foot faltered, but there was no graceful way to escape. When we came within speaking distance of each other he blushed and with a sheepish grin said theatrically, "Dah-ling, say something to me in tongues." Not many had the presence of mind to cover their awkwardness with such good humor.

There was a new image foisted upon me and it came as quite a shock, because practically none of the criticisms leveled at my personal pentecostalism were appropriate. My guilt was by association only. I was not an ecstatic—or a pietist, or moral perfectionist. And having never, to my recollection, heard the sound of unknown tongues before those moments of intensity with Dave Wilkerson at Poughkeepsie, I had had no experience of glossalalia until several weeks after I was immersed in the power and love of God the Spirit. When I finally received the gift, my earnest seeking after it was out of deference to so many new friends whose doctrine denied Spirit-baptism without it. There was nothing to lose, and much to be gained by setting them at ease, but I had had no doubts concerning my baptism in the

108

Spirit from the time Dave Wilkerson said, "The baptizer's here, we can leave."

However, the Lord had more in mind than smiting the faint-hearted with scurrying rumors when He devised such a careful plan of signs and wondermongering to broadcast my pentecostal stance. He was gathering for Himself a body of people to be powerful evidence of His Son's life in Houston's East End. With a frequency that increased rapidly over the passing weeks, all sorts and conditions of God's people presented themselves at the rectory door professing boldly their calling to associate with my ministry.

And what an unlikely crew they appeared to be! There were those whose opinions about an "Episcopalians' kind of man" were less than charitable, to say the least. Some of these had clear vision and were more or less defensible in their complaints of hypocrisy and ecclesiasticism. The rest were petty heretics. There were those, too—already Episco-palians or other main-line denominationalists—who were driven by disillusionment to the fringes of the Church. Some were stable leaders whose souls were tinder ready to be sparked, but most were mere malcontents. It took about six months between October '64 and April '65 to sort things out. To begin with there was no way to judge who was called and who was not, but I sensed that, somewhere in the midst of that motley crew, God had sown the seed of a renewed Redeemer Church.

Meanwhile, however, I experienced the most hectic half year of my life—with the possible exception of the same period of time during the previous year when I had been swamped with hordes of unruly youngsters.

It would be difficult to assess fairly the sorts of persons generally attracted to miracles, because their lives have so little in common. Our growing charismatic community missed nothing: curiosity seekers, opportunists, spiritual gadflies, self-appointed prophets, skeptics, impotents, mega-lomaniacs—as well as the genuinely disillusioned and those who seek after truth. For six months my life and ministry

109

were overwhelmed by them. A few parishioners with linger-ing but vain hopes of restoring traditional Episcopalianism to Redeemer Church were dismayed at the calibre of their new brothers. One of them carried the matter all the way to the Presiding Bishop's office. "What right have you, sir," I have been told she demanded, "to ask for our money when you're giving perfectly good Episcopal churches away to Pentecostals?" However, those were the last gasps of tradi-tionalism.

Although still convinced of my calling to the Episcopal priesthood, by January 1965 I had sloughed off the last vestiges of Episcopalianism. Which is not to suggest that I took license with canon law or with my ordination vows, or that, as far as I could see, my beliefs were at variance with the Book of Common Prayer and the creeds. What I mean is this, that mere traditionalism and empty form (and I was astounded to discover the extent of my dependency on these for a sense of leadership in liturgy) were called into question by an earnest desire to act only out of personal obedience, and they were being systematically replaced by simple and forthright expressions of the Sonship life I was walking in. I was not tempted to abandon all at once the forms and formulas of my old habits and, as it were, stand ritually naked, waiting for a better clothing, but one by one the unquestioned and the assumed were challenged and dealt with. I suppose it must be said that in the light of my new-found freedom I was willing to fly even in the face of prior commitments, had I clearly heard God require it of me; but that never happened, nor did I expect it to, because I felt called both to be free from Episcopalianism and to serve as an Episcopal priest. Such a conundrum only God's grace could solve, and I was willing to trust Him for it.

I recall sharing these thoughts with a friend once. The pressure of 'come-out-from-among-them-ism' was a burning issue in so many minds in those days, that I frequently had to defend even the possibility of a true calling from God to remain within the confines of a structured organization. At the end of our discussion my friend said, "Graham, you haven't been delivered out of the Episcopal Church, the Episcopal Church has been delivered out of you." That summary satisfied my soul then, and it still does. So the issues of usefulness and propriety, and considerations of whether a thing was right or acceptable, were no longer a matter of concern to me. My whole being was irreversibly fixed upon faithfulness and submission to a God in heaven who was revealing His pleasure to me step by step. That was enough for me to handle at the moment.

For several months in 1964 the enormous weight of sin and suffering in the lives of a great number of Houston's East-Enders had become mine; during a lenten despair God broke me under the burden of it. Then during Eastertide I caught a new vision of His Church. It was not a dream, but a prophetic vision; neither the force of traditionalism nor the opinions of latecomers would be able to draw my sights aside, because while sharing with me the secrets of His earthly kingdom, He filled me with an enormous love for Himself. As time progressed the burden grew lighter, but it has not lifted; the vision has moved away into a better perspective, but it has never dimmed. In fact, the vision of the body of Christ with which I was surprisingly graced during the latter moments of my soul's travail in 1964 grew richer, not poorer. It was then mere skin and bone, growing later into full flesh. During 1965, through the contributions of two of God's most wholesome saints—both faithful servants whom I loved as my own soul—there was added a dimension of radical faith and the postulate of life lived wholly in worship and praise.

Both Earle Frid and George Bostrom were associated with a small independent full-gospel church on Houston's north side. Although officially it bore a complicated name, we called it simply Grace Chapel.

The original congregation of Grace Chapel was Chinese-American, as were the pastor, Hong Sit, and most of the elders. When we first became acquainted with them, the

111

membership—I should say 'fellowship' because they disavowed any membership—was about fifty percent oriental. Their shepherd was on a missionary tour of China, and Brother George was ministering in an interim capacity during his absence. Brother Earle, a revered elder member who was one of the few hoary heads in sight, had found himself serving in a position similar to Brother George's when a year or so earlier the struggling little flock first began to grow. Under Earle's leadership they stepped out in a venture of faith and constructed with their own hands a building to house the voice of their gentle praises.

And their praises were most gentle and ever so childlike in expression! Never before had I experienced the simplicity and spontaneity of worship that breathed in the presence of those kindly, self-effacing orientals. There was peace and so much assurance of God's mercy in the manner of their singing and prayers, that I often stood weeping with joy while the Spirit of God's tender love drew me close in adoration. I use the plural 'we' when remembering the little church because by a strange happenstance of God's sovereignty, most of those who had gathered around my ministry across town in Redeemer parish found themselves enjoying Grace Chapel's fellowship with informal regularity every Wednesday and Sunday night. We arranged our own nighttime meetings on Tuesday and Friday so as not to interfere.

From the beginning I sensed that our relationship to the tiny Chinese-American sister congregation was a temporary one of hospitality on their part in the face of need on ours; and it was the openness of heart and magnanimity of spirit in Brother George Bostrom's ministry that drew us close in Christ in worship, and freed us from ourselves for praise. If I had any doubt that God had engineered the temporary union of these two fellowships, it was dispelled the moment Brother George opened his mouth to teach. Week after week from the lips of a guileless man who was ignorant of our liturgical lectionary, I heard expository sermons and words of inspiration covering the same themes (and often from the very same scriptures) about which the Spirit of God had instructed us that morning from our own epistle and gospel. That was a little sign of God's favor, but a great encouragement.

It was here in Grace Chapel that I first heard prophecy directed to a specific circumstance of my own life. I realize what a puzzling statement that must be to one who has never heard prophecy on the lips of a contemporary, or who ignorantly thinks that preaching and prophesying are synonymous endeavors. I was at that place myself until seven years ago and then not really concerned about the matter; the office and function of prophet—even among the great classical seers of Israel—had always been an enigma to me. My imagination stumbled when I thought of them as personalities who had wives and children and neighbors; it had simply never occurred to me that there could be prophets alive today—charlatans maybe, but not the real thing. One night when the Wednesday prayer service was over I was sitting quietly where I had been all evening. A man whose name and face I cannot now remember laid his hands upon my shoulder and began to speak softly but forcefully. I looked about to see whether he was reading the words I heard—they had such a ring of authenticity—but his eyes were shut and he seemed unaware of me.

Yes, my beloved, I have called you and I have set you in that place of my choosing where you will be to me a most gracious servant. Speak boldly the words I will put in your mouth, and do only my pleasure in the thing that you do. I have chosen you, you have not chosen me. I will keep and guide you in the way that you go, and I will be in the way also, to speak to you and comfort you in your distresses. But be not afraid nor dismayed for I will be with you even in dark places, and in places where your understanding and vision fail: I am the Lord. My words will give light to your path and strength to your spirit; heed them well, and obey.

You shall lead my people and be a gatherer of my scattered ones. My people perish, for my ways and even

I myself have vanished from before their eyes, and in ignorance they seek here and there but find nothing to satisfy their soul's hunger. Many shall come to you for wisdom and counsel; but they shall hear me even in your words, and they shall see me even in your eyes, and they shall know me even in your love. I am God, walk humbly with me. I am the Lord, wait patiently upon me. Yea, I am the Lord, the Holy one of Israel who has called you.

I was awe-struck.

Those around us who overheard were hushed, and when he finished speaking there was a general lisping of "Praise the Lord" and "Thank you, Jesus." The unassuming man walked away without another word.

God had spoken and said those things personally to me, and to me only! And His prophet had vanished in the crowd of unfamiliar faces. What a strange new world I was in.

I knew that God had showered the force and authority of that prophetic statement on me, but I recognized also the hideous danger I could be in. If God had not said those things and in that way, then I was a severely unbalanced man and ultimately would prove to be a menace. But I trusted Him and told no one of the prophecy or my doubts concerning it for many months.

In January 1965 a member of Redeemer Church who was also one of the charismatic band came to me following the Sunday Eucharist. It was the morning when newly elected vestrymen were instituted. "Graham," he said, "while you were praying for the new vestrymen I think the Lord gave me a prophecy. I sure had a strong impression to speak out, but I knew that would cause confusion so I wrote it down on my order of service."

"Let's see it," I requested eagerly.

"Well, my writing's bad, let me read it," he said.

The burden of the message was a word of encouragement that the 1965 vestry was a body of the Lord's choosing which He would guide and protect. But it went on to speak to one

114

addressed more personally. It concluded, "I have chosen and called you to be a pastor of my pastors."

"I think that last part's for you," he said.

"Well ... I suppose so," I commented. "But since it's coupled with those remarks about the vestry, it probably just means the congregation's going to follow my leadership this year. That's good news."

"How many pastors are there here?" he asked pointedly, placing his finger on the sentence referring to pastors. "I think it means you'll be a Bishop."

I smiled. "Not much chance of my being a Bishop in the Episcopal Church at this point. Maybe one day the Lord's going to put me in the position of helping other pastors," I volunteered.

"At least that," he said cryptically.

I had once again the uncomfortable feeling that these thoughts could be the vain imaginings of well-meaning flatterers, and not prophecy at all. How easily my head could be turned! When the words were spoken they were heard as the authentic voice of God. But the content! Good gracious.

I went to the basement chapel to pray. The second chapter of Ezekiel was impressed on my mind and turning to the Bible I scanned the first few words. Suddenly I was on my feet, feeling strangely buoyant as though lifted into a standing position by an invisible force. A tremendous sense of God's presence enveloped me and I read aloud.

And he said to me, "Son of man, stand upon your feet, and I will speak with you." And when he spoke to me, the Spirit entered into me and set me upon my feet; and I heard him speaking to me. And he said to me, "Son of man, I send you to the people of Israel, to a nation of rebels, who have rebelled against me; they and their fathers have transgressed against me to this very day. The people also are impudent and stubborn: I send you to them; and you shall say to them, 'Thus says the Lord God.' And whether they hear or refuse to hear (for they are a rebellious house) they will know that there has been a prophet among them. And you, son of man, be not afraid of them, nor be afraid of their words, though briers and thorns are with you and you sit upon scorpions; be not afraid of their words, nor be dismayed at their looks, for they are a rebellious house. And you shall speak my words to them, whether they hear or refuse to hear; for they are a rebellious house.

"But you, son of man, hear what I say to you; be not rebellious like that rebellious house; open your mouth, and eat what I give you." And when I looked, behold, a hand was stretched out to me, and, lo, a written scroll was in it; and he spread it before me; and it had writing on the front and on the back, and there were written on it words of lamentation and mourning and woe.

And he said to me, "Son of man, eat what is offered to you; eat this scroll, and go, speak to the house of Israel. So I opened my mouth, and he gave me the scroll to eat. And he said to me, "Son of man, eat this scroll that I give you and fill your stomach with it." Then I ate it; and it was in my mouth as sweet as honey.

And he said to me, "Son of man, go, get you to the house of Israel, and speak with my words to them. For you are not sent to a people of foreign speech and a hard language, but to the house of Israel——

(Ezekiel 2:1–3:5)

All my doubts concerning the prophecy were removed.

Early in November 1964 I confided in Earle Frid my fears concerning our ignorance of the content of scripture. "We've started a Tuesday night prayer meeting, Brother Earle, but I'm as new as they are about what God has to say on most things. How can I help them?"

His answer was as direct as his marvelous Christian witness. "That's simple, invite me to teach you."

"You're invited," I said.

"I accept on one condition," he warned. "That I be free to teach exactly what the Bible says whether the Episcopal Church agrees or not."

"Agreed," I marvelled that there was not the slightest qualm in my use of that word.

Brother Earle began teaching on Tuesday nights. Eventu-

116

ally he held forth on two nights a week, and then after a while he was teaching on Sunday mornings also. There were a few arguments from old timers about having a Baptist in so key a parish position, but in the light of his message their complaints seemed insignificant to me. It was a powerful teaching about having faith in every word of scripture that God says to His servants, and it brought refreshing simplicity to our concept of obedience, focusing judgment on every facet of the totally committed Christian life. Meeting after meeting we shared happily in the great and small miracles, and the wonders that God was doing every day in our lives; and while the testimony of plainly answered prayer was mounting, faith was being built to a high pitch of expectancy. The supernatural was becoming a normal way of looking at things for us. It was not news that God could do anything He willed to do, but it was an entirely new idea that for those who walk close at His heels, He does what they ask of Him. I remembered my earlier thoughts about Dave Wilkerson, and realized a faith like his had now been planted in me. I marvelled at the mystery; we were experiencing for the first time the revelation of the power of faith in the lives of those who walk close to the living God.

I recall an incident that typifies the peak of expectancy to which faith had matured during those six months preceding Easter 1965. Two couples from a town about forty miles from Houston had begun attending our night meetings. One of them was under deep conviction concerning their calling to a charismatic life; the other's enthusiasm lagged behind, but they were not so much balky as careful. They were realizing what a serious business it was to fall into the hands of the living God. In the course of his teaching one night, Brother Earle shared a delightful testimony that brought the couple up short in their flagging enthusiasm. It was the story of a simple lady missionary in Canada's prairie provinces. She traveled hundreds of miles each Sunday to meet commitments to outlying congregations where she labored as an evangelist among children. One Sunday, in a press of time,

117

she was hurrying down a lonely Alberta highway to the next station. Hearing a thumping in one of her tires and seeing plain evidence of a blow-out, she stopped and spoke plainly, though respectfully: "Lord, I am Thy servant, and I am about Thy business. Thou knowest the great need of these children for proper instruction, and Thou knowest I have no time for delay. I trust that Thou wilt repair this tire instantly and I shall go about my task unhindered. Lord, I would remind Thee, Thou hast promised that if I ask anything of the Father in Thy name, He will give it to me, and so I ask Thee Father, in the name of Thy Son, Jesus, Amen." She held her open Bible up to the Lord for Him to see—just a reminder that it was His word and not hers. She started her car and drove on. There was no sign of a flat tire.

The next Tuesday night was a time of excitement for the young couples. That day the withholding pair had revealed their desire for prayer to receive the baptism of the Spirit, but everything went wrong at the time of their departure for the prayer meeting. At the last moment the baby sitter was unable to come, the children were fussy, and one of the men was late in returning from work. Finally they left home a half hour after the meeting had begun in Houston. About ten miles down the road there was a bumping in their front tire and obvious signs of a flat. How exasperating! However, stopping by the roadside they decided to pray, "Lord, you did it for that lady missionary in Canada, and we're your servants, too. We know you want us to be at the meeting tonight so please heal that tire and get us there before everything's over. In Jesus' name. Amen."

They started the car and drove without any trouble to Houston where the young couple received the baptism of the Spirit that night. On the way home, rejoicing, they felt a sudden jar. The tire went flat and had to be replaced by the roadside.

XII

*You Shall Receive the
Gift of the Holy Spirit.*
(Acts 2:38)

Mounting the pulpit, I scanned what seemed to be two hundred and fifty faces before bowing my head and bidding them to prayer; then there was a brief moment of silence in which my thoughts waited for words. Taking advantage of the void, my mind's eye focused on one of the faces perceived in that fleeting glance, and I struggled to remember where I had seen it before.

There he is, I thought, as recognition dawned, *right in the middle of the congregation, big as life.*

My gratitude went out to the Rector of Galveston's Grace Church for including me in a lenten series of guest preachers; it was the first such invitation I had received since being baptized with the Spirit eight months earlier. A sharing of some of my current testimony went well and there was an almost tangible drawing together in expectant faith toward the close of the service.

When the ushers came forward for the alms basins, and the organist's improvizations signaled a pause in the service, I gave thought to the man in the pew. He was sitting by his wife. From my vantage point in the pulpit earlier I had seen crutches propped against the pew. The couple's name was Uher, and only the night before he had challenged me vigorously after our prayer meeting in Houston. He was not unpleasant, but he was forthright and a bit too agressive in his quest for honesty. The Uhers had come all the way from Galveston to our prayer meeting and that night it had been especially alive with testimonies of healings and miracles. As usual, at the close of the meeting I started toward the chapel where prayer would be offered at the specific request of those who came for it, but Mr. Uher intercepted me in the hallway.

"You know," he began, appearing agitated but under control, "I sure believe that God heals and all that, but I think they're making up an awful lot of that stuff they said in there."

"Oh, no," I responded in surprise. "What makes you think so?"

"I don't know," he said. "That's too much. If you have a headache—take an aspirin, that's what they're for. All this business about trusting God for everything! It makes me feel funny."

I knew what he meant. There had been a couple of testimonies in which people claimed healing "by faith." They had meant well; which is to say they trusted God to do it eventually, but I admit it sounded to the practical mind like pretending a bit. One person testified to a healing that obviously was not yet complete: she was a young girl who claimed her eyes were healed. Having discarded her glasses in an attempt to demonstrate confidence in the healing power of faith, she asked us to join her in giving thanks. Then she shared a verse from the Bible, and the force of her testimony was lost in ugly squinting and an embarassing display of word-stumbling. Later in private I pointed out that when the healing of her eyes was complete she would not be able to wear glasses, but until then she was unwise to go without them. "And besides," I said, "it looks like pretense."

However, there had been so many other instances of healing that were authentic. *What was his trouble anyway?* I wondered. "Listen," I said, "several of those stories were clearly true, I don't think it's fair to discount them because of the others."

"There wasn't one clinically-proved healing mentioned, was there?" he punctuated his words for emphasis, "and you can talk all you like about dramatic healings, but you can't show one to me right now, can you?"

I shrugged and turned toward the chapel, remembering Jesus' temptation in the desert. *If you're the son of God, go to the chapel and heal someone right now!* I felt a strange voice tempt me.

My reveries of the previous night in Houston were disturbed by the dirge-like pace of a closing hymn. While we were still singing, the Rector approached me to suggest we invite the congregation to remain for prayer and the laying on of hands. I concurred. After the invitation was extended, about three-quarters of the congregation remained behind and a few of them began straggling forward for ministry.

At my request, two laymen joined us behind the altar rail. One was a lawyer and the other a medical doctor—both lived in Galveston County, but recently had become new members of Redeemer Church, Houston. Mrs. Uher, with one foot greatly enlarged and swathed in bandages, hobbled on her crutches to the altar rail and knelt down. I was excited when I saw her coming forward, and I remarked to myself how that circumstance might easily have produced dread.

What a set up, I thought. *Someone's going to look the fool tonight, either me or Mr. Uher.*

My eagerness to pray for the woman was preempted by the doctor who began speaking the moment we laid hands on her. In the middle of his words I suddenly touched his hand. His eyes had been closed so he opened them and silently quizzed me with his upraised brows.

"There's no need to say any more, Bob," I said confidently, "she's healed."

And she was.

As soon as he had begun praying, something—is it too fanciful to say "someone"?—inside me began leaping up and down, and shouting, *"She's healed! she's healed! she's healed!"*

I said to the woman, "Ma'am, that foot's all well, you can return to your seat if you like." She walked back to the pew as gracefully as possible and her crutches remained in the choir area in mute testimony to the power of God.

It was very apparent upon her return to the center aisle, that the only difficulty she had in walking was caused by the bandage. When she moved swiftly down the choir steps, the congregation gasped and broke into a confusion of whispers. But through the hushed babble a child's high pitched voice exclaimed with delight, "Mommy, Daddy, Jesus is real!"

That night a great many people, including the little girl and her entire family, came to a personal awareness of the risen Lord Jesus; and afterwards at the lawyer's home, several more received the baptism with the Holy Spirit.

Later I learned the rest of the story about the Uhers. They had returned to Galveston the night before in a cold spring drizzle. Mrs. Uher slipped on the porch of her own home, and twisting an ankle, fell on it. In no time the joint was huge and discolored. X-rays revealed there were no fractures, but ligaments were torn and the ankle was severely sprained.

That incident represented a significant turning point in ministry for me. Only a subtle change occurred in my point of view, but eventually it was to have far-reaching consequences. Until then I had relied heavily on the experience of others for the strength of what little confidence I found in exercising ministry gifts of the Spirit such as healing, miracles, and prophesy. I had seen many strange wonders. However, from the beginning they were obviously sovereign acts of God—that is, He had approached me obliquely, as it were, and I saw curious signs of His power follow in my wake. Then my ministry became associated with other charismatics, and people began seeking me out as one to whom

122

they might come with expectation of having prayers answered. I had not felt competent in this even though I was willing to give public witness to my faith and confidence in the charismatic gifts. There is a vast difference between looking behind yourself to see what God has miraculously done and looking ahead to see what He is sending for *you* to accomplish in the power of His name.

After every nighttime service Earle Frid, four other men, and I, went to the basement chapel and prayed for people with specific needs; that prayer time was unrehearsed and the requests were presented *ad lib* by those assembled. Night after night, simple faith brought forth the most astonishing evidence of God's mercy and power; bones were healed, sight restored, and lives mended. Seldom were we finished before midnight.

In those after-hour meetings I was well aware of my dependence on Brother Earle. His comfortable presence allowed me freedom and confidence to speak of the validity of charismatic gifts with a growing assurance. Often the things I said were a source of faith in the suppliant and Earle would add nothing, but even at those times I was conscious of his firm support and encouragement. I knew Earle was a gift to me, a brother who would lovingly share his confidence in the faith of the Son of God until my own grew to a better use.

A similar circumstance prevailed at Grace Chapel. Each Wednesday and Sunday night Brother George Bostrom (together with Brother Earle, who was usually present too) invited me to share in the ministry of the laying on of hands at the close of their services. I became free to minister, knowing that any deficiency of mine would be covered by the enabling of others.

In these two settings the struggling band of charismatics associated with my ministry experienced for several months a sustained level of faith to see miracles happen, and we found in our worship a freedom and fluency of praise that was compelling and powerful. However, in the spring of

1965 I began sensing something that saddened and distressed me at first.

God had placed a comfortable unity between our growing charismatic fellowship and Grace Chapel under George Bostrom's ministry. Then Brother George stepped down from his interim post, and the leadership reverted to Hong Sit, whose mission in China was ended. Imperceptibly our relationship to the oriental church changed. At first I accused myself, but it was soon quite plain that the intense bond between us had been broken. The breach was not because we were at odds with each other; there was no unkindness or enmity of any sort: God had given, and He had taken away. There was a bland friendly relationship where once there had been ardent involvement. Looking back I recognize that it was George Bostrom's ministry which had been God's design in bringing us to Grace Chapel. There, under a powerful anointing, we learned freedom in praise, and well ordered joy in the giving of our thanks, and we learned to be gentle and quiet in our enthusiasm.

One evening after supper Betty was holding our two-year-old daughter Jane in her lap while thumbing through a magazine in search of amusing pictures. They came across an advertisement for overseas relief funds that portrayed a little oriental girl looking at the viewer with pleading eyes. Jane brightened when she saw the child and exclaimed in her childish tongue, "Dat's a praise de Lord!" I, too, found the compelling feature in my experience of the little Chinese-American church to be praise, and beginning early in March 1965, I had a recurring thought. It was "community of praise." To my knowledge that phrase was entirely new to me, but as the months progressed toward 1966 it took on an unusual nuance of meaning.

On Shrove Tuesday after the chapel service I looked at Arabella Miner, one of the young single women who was among the first to be attracted by signs and wonders, and I knew she had something on her mind.

"Arabella," I said, "you have something you want to talk about, don't you?"

"Do I?" was her half serious reply. "I didn't think so."

"Looks to me like you do. Why don't we talk Thursday after Choir rehearsal."

"Sure," she shrugged nonchalantly.

When we were seated in the chapel on Thursday night, Arabella began to talk. She prefaced her statements with "Graham, I've never thought this before, but . . ." or "I don't know where this idea's coming from, but. . . ." It was plain that her thoughts involved some fresh inspiration; usually so staid, she was alive and bristling. The ideas presented were not complicated, only radical from the point of view of the established Church. Although they were new to her they were several months old to me.

"We need to live together—all of us," she said. "We need to learn how to save money and time and effort by living together and sharing everything, because God wants to do something unusual with us. We could take that old apartment building across the street and fix it up for all of us to live in. You know, if we're ever really going to be the church, I mean, *really*, then we're going to have to live together somehow."

I showed Arabella the second chapter of Acts and she got even more excited.

"Arabella," I said, sharing her excitement, "The Lord's been talking to me about that for several months now, and a few weeks ago Bob Eckert had the same ideas. Let's pray about it through lent and see what we come up with after Easter, Okay?"

As I have said, the Galveston incident during lent was a turning point. From that moment onward there began to be a greater self-confidence among the inner core of Redeemer's charismatic fellowship—a confidence, that is, to minister to others and to lead an assembly in spontaneous utterances of praise and worship. Personally, I felt a growing confidence in my own leadership and recognized that not only

his own confidence grows

had there been a healthy dependence on the spiritual strength of Grace Chapel's ministers, but also in me there was a cowardly dependence on them: I was fearful of taking initiative in their presence. Being raised and trained in a formalistic religious environment, I was like a stricken doe by the roadside. When confronted with free worship, the slightest sound of harsh criticism would have sent me scurrying to the shelter of liturgies and formulas; but under Brother George's sensitive leadership, the little Chinese flock had been an obedient vessel of God's grace to lead a fellow servant to freedom.

Then God's work in that relationship was finished. The sensitivity ceased and I found myself withholding thoughts and feelings from them because I knew they were ideas which were at variance with the fundamentalist doctrine of their pastor and elders. So, even though there was cordial sharing of ourselves in spiritual union with Grace Chapel until well into 1966, the commonality of our minds and souls had been withdrawn after the previous Easter.

Brother Earle and I had a falling out, too. It was over my vision of a renewed Episcopal Church; he did not share the denominational emphasis. Our relationship took on a growing tension, and we were both uncomfortable until the spring of 1965 when Earle and his wife Ethel returned to Canada.

We were on our own.

In the Acts of the Apostles there is evidence that the operation of the early church expanded after persecution. Those who were clinging too tightly to one another were scattered. At Redeemer Church, Houston, the opposite occurred. God drove a tiny core of charismatics into the shelter of one another's arms by scattering from their midst those who lacked as broad a vision of their common calling and as deep a personal commitment to it. Many, who had associated themselves with our fellowship because of an affinity to the Grace Chapel environment, slowly withdrew as the bond between the two groups was severed. There were a great many whose kinship to us was centered upon the remarkable

126

reproduction from Grace Church

charisma of Brother Earle's teaching. When he left, so did they. What resulted was a tiny band of stalwart visionaries who clung to one another like frightened children lost in the dark. By God's grace we had been given to one another and the bond of our common love was stronger than nuptial ties. We were unconditionally and irreversibly committed in love to be the instrument of God's charismatic power for the renewal of Redeemer Church. There were less than three dozen souls, men, women, and children, and somehow the thought was implanted in our minds that we were "the minister." My relation to the group was unusual because I was an Episcopal priest, but otherwise *we* were the minister, and I gladly shared the burden.

Arabella and I talked after the scheduled communion service on Good Friday.

"I've just been talking to Nancy," she volunteered, "and I think the Lord wants everyone who will do it to come together daily to search the scriptures and worship like we've experienced it out at Grace Chapel. And He wants us to find a way to live closer together so we can share our lives too."

"Amen," I said. "Bob and I just said the same thing to each other last night. The Lord also told us what time to get together every day. What's He said to you?"

She feigned a look of rebuke. "Five-thirty A.M."

"Exactly," I concurred.

We began daily meetings at five-thirty in the morning on Easter Monday, 1965. Dr. Bob Eckert drove back and forth forty miles from Galveston County; John Grimmet, a laborer, stopped off on his way to work; so did Ladd Fields, an engineer for an instrument manufacturer. Jerry Barker, a Galveston lawyer, came as often as he could. Although Jerry and Esther were personally committed from the start, it was not until the following summer, when his tentative plans for entering seminary were changed, that they made their commitment to the Redeemer fellowship without reservation. Three single young women—a teacher, a librarian, and a medical editor, traveled a dozen or so miles across town from their suburban apartments. The schedule was easiest on me; I lived next door at the rectory.

That was the beginning.

For six months thirty-one people all but lived together. In order to include wives and children in this fellowship, husbands continued at the early morning hour and returned at 7:30 in the evening for a family gathering. All day Saturday, and Sunday after church, were spent together in one of the member's homes. Although nothing formal was put forward and no covenants were signed, each family let me know that everything they had or could command was at the disposal of the ministry—savings, insurance, earnings, possessions, borrowing power, themselves; we relinquished everything in a literal way. It was made available to help the needy.

During that six months the fame of miracles ceased. Miracles did not, but the fame did. No longer were people presenting themselves to become a part of Redeemer's charismatic group. Our program was too rigorous for most, and our commitment was radical to say the least, but also, the signs and wonders were no longer in public display. Instead, God began a deep work among us. It was a work of informal teaching in matters of discipleship. We had counted the cost and paid the price; now we were learning the ropes.

And oh, how we loved one another! An amazing act of God's graciousness drew us together in a bond of tender affection and mutual concern. We grew sensitive to each other's simplest needs and quite frankly shared our feelings in frequent, open embraces.

The greatest lesson we learned was about the gentle care that God has for His servants. Our children contracted disease along with their schoolmates, for example, but they seldom had them for longer than overnight; our prayers brought about the healing of such things as measles and mumps in less than half a day.

Also we learned about trust. When school was out in May, everyone moved in close to the church. It was no mean feat for a doctor to sell his practice and his home in a quiet little town and move into a small two bedroom apartment in Houston's busy East End. Nor did the lawyer find it any easier, but by August 1965, all thirty-one of us were living within three blocks of each other. During that summer we joined together nightly in the basement chapel and shared the wonderful things God was doing in our families' lives.

One day that summer, our son Nathan, then six, was thrown while playing. He landed on his knee at the corner of a concrete curbing. In no time the knee was swollen and black. He came screaming into the house, hopping on one foot. Betty and I prayed for him and then suggested we call Dr. Eckert so the knee could be X-rayed. Nathan said, "Didn't we ask Jesus to heal it?"

"Yes," I answered confidently.

"Has he done it?" the boy asked.

"Yes," I said with hesitation, "but it isn't finished yet. He's taken away most of the pain, but we need to have Dr. Eckert look at it, Nathan."

"No, He healed it, we don't have to do any more," he asserted.

I was nonplussed. Betty suggested we wait until he got bored with immobility or had knocked his knee and wearied of the pain. She was confident he would ask for the medical help before long. Days passed and he still insisted that Jesus had healed it. There was no doubt in Dr. Eckert's mind that the knee cap was broken when he saw Nathan non-professionally, but the child valiantly walked and played stiff-legged. Every time we saw him coddling the knee we reminded him that it could be bandaged and there were pain killers to make the healing easy. He insisted that Jesus had healed it.

Betty's mother from North Carolina was visiting us at the time. She was deeply offended that we had not taken Nathan to the doctor whether he wanted to go or not. "He's too young to make that decision," she emphasized, "and besides, every child wants to avoid having shots. He's just trying to play it safe."

On the following Tuesday night Nathan's Sunday-school

129

teacher, John Grimmet, carried the crippled boy from his bed to the chapel after we had spent the evening there in prayer. Pajama-clad and tiny among several adults, he was reclining comfortably with his damaged knee outstretched on the pew. We prayed. What others' hearts were asking I was not aware, but I was asking God to heal him. When I looked at his small form to see whether he was getting tired, I was moved to tears. He had raised his hands and with his eyes closed and his face tilted heavenward, Nathan was praying in tongues quietly to himself. He had received his baptism with the Holy Spirit.

A couple of days later Betty's mother prepared to return home. She took Betty aside and spoke her mind unequivocably on the subject of Nathan's knee. "He'll grow up to be a cripple and you'll regret it always," she warned. Betty came to me and suggested we take him to the doctor no matter what his own wishes were. I was about to agree when the Lord spoke to me. *"Which would you rather, that he have a crippled leg or a crippled faith?"*

"Betty," I said, "as long as Nathan believes that Jesus has healed his knee, and he feels no need to go to the doctor, I think we should honor his faith, foolish or not."

The chagrined grandmother left the next morning. That same evening Nathan's knee was completely normal and without pain. We thanked the Lord Jesus for His faithfulness.

"And a little child will lead them."

Betty and I recognized it was our faith that had been tested, and we had come uncomfortably close to failing.

The charismatic corps had learned most of its lessons well by the fall of 1965, when there was once again an upsurge of interest in our corporate life. We had been gathered together under the covert of a loving Father's wings; resting there in faith we had grown stronger in grace each day. Finally the life that had been maturing in us became a source of power for others and a magnificent plan of communal sharing and

130

sacrificial servanthood began to unfold. Redeemer Church's corporate renewal was under way. It was only a bud; the full bloom is a parish whose corporate life and ministry of social concern are astonishing emblems of the grace and dominion of Jesus Christ in a troubled time.

*   *   *

Grant, we beseech thee, merciful God, that thy Church, being gathered together in unity by the Holy Spirit, may manifest thy power among all peoples, to the glory of Thy Name; through Jesus Christ our Lord, who liveth and reigneth with thee and the same Spirit, one God, world without end. Amen.*

*Book of Common Prayer, 1928, p. 185.

Interlude

"Dear Parishioners:

"Last week I lived one of the fullest and most treasured weeks of my life. I was at the Church of the Redeemer (Houston, Texas). ... The Church of the Redeemer has had a most profound influence on my way of thinking as a Christian, as a Catholic, and as a Catholic priest. ... How do I describe the Redeemer experience? For me it is an experience of 'the body of Christ.' Or it is the experience of Jesus Christ in His body ... ?

"A believing Christian finds the experience of Jesus Christ very real and tangible when observing and participating in the love that the members of a parish family like Redeemer have for one another. ... What is the secret of such a loving community (body) of Christ at this parish? It is not that these people just happen to be naturally extraordinary people. They are not. The parish represents a cross-section of Americana. The secret lies in the transforming and empowering love of a Father who calls us through His Son in the Holy Spirit to be His people. The 'body of Christ,' of which every parish is meant to be the local embodiment, is not of human making in the sense that if we just try hard enough with human power it is bound to happen. It is of divine making. We must be generous and willing servants of the

133

Lord Jesus who, through his Spirit (Holy Spirit) working in each of us according to His gifts, will build us up into His body. . . ."

Father James W. Scheuer, co-pastor of Holy Spirit Roman Catholic Church in Virginia, Minnesota, wrote these words in his weekly parish bulletin on February 6, 1972. If you have given the preceding chapters even casual credence, you will understand my amazement that such a thing could happen.

I wrote in the prelude to this book that its several chapters would pick up the threads of certain human lives and re-count how God the Holy Spirit wove them into a fabric—and a goodly cloth it has been, too—for the fashioning of a garment of praise. That habiliment was the experience Father Scheuer described to his parishioners.

On the day after Christmas in 1969, *Time* magazine's assessment of the previous decade singled out a handful of viable Christian ministries that seemed likely, they thought, to be models for the Church of the '70's. They marvelled at the religious initiative displayed by certain "youthful dispos-sessed" and at the upsurge of communalism. Their writer penned, "the commune is an authentic American tradition, dating principally from the 19th century. Young and old are again attempting the collective life, particularly in several urban communities.

"An Episcopal pentecostalist is having remarkable success with one such experiment in Houston. Some 120 followers of the Rev. Graham Pulkingham have organized 16 experimen-tal communes ranging from groups of working people to öster homes for parentless children. The communes are set up in ordinary houses scattered throughout the city. . . ."

In 1969 there was nothing experimental about the 16 or more communes associated with the Church of the Re-deemer, nor were their inhabitants in any sense my follow-ers. They were our homes, our life circumstance, and each of them was the result of an expedient for ministry. That is to

134

Households

say, we opened ourselves to those whom God sent for heal-ing, whatever their condition in body, .mind, or spirit. Our homes, our family life, our savings and earnings, our prayers and compassion, were offered freely as instruments of grace to effect whatever in His mercy God saw fit to require of us. He required much—in fact, He required all. Presently there are forty such communes involving more than three hundred and fifty persons in the fellowship of the Redeemer parish. They are still our homes even though we have evolved com-munal groups whose expansion by-passed the rigid struc-tures of the natural family unit. These healing households, as we prefer to call them, have become productive training grounds for the young to mature in ministry and they have been fruitful environments of healing and rehabilitation for hundreds of persons whose condition was otherwise hope-less.

On Pentecost in 1971, CBS television gave nationwide exposure to an hour-long religious documentary called "Following the Spirit." It was a sympathetic portrayal of the "liturgical way of life" in Houston's Episcopal Church of the Redeemer, faithfully reporting an obvious charisma of praise and love. In a press release the show's producer, Ted Holmes, expressed the opinion that Redeemer Church is "the most exciting and vital example of the new religious way to be found in the country today. These people are living together, working together, dedicating themselves to the ministries of the church. It is not a commune—a com-mune implies dropping out. The fellowship members have not turned their backs on society. On the contrary, they are trying to make changes in society at large and particularly in the Houston area by setting an example for others to follow."

Guideposts' magazine is constantly searching for congre-gations that are dedicated to their calling with imagination and energy that is clearly beyond normal. Annually one of

135

them is selected for citation in the magazine, and the members receive an award and commendation for their particular contribution to America's religious life. Redeemer Church was chosen in 1972. The citation in *Guideposts'* March 1972 issue concludes with these words:

> The Church of the Redeemer's outreach is strong and growing. But it is important to realize that while these committed parishioners want their church to be a center of renewal for different kinds of Christians from every denomination, they hold firmly to the idea of a strong parish church. Every member of the congregation feels himself responsible to the Lord for his own individual life of faith, but all congregants will tell you that the Christian life was meant to be a corporate experience, that the Lord truly uses individuals, but He uses them best when they are bound together in faithful and loving harmony.
>
> By their example, the members of the congregation of the Church of the Redeemer are strengthening the concept of church, the concept of a body of believers. Their strong, innovative, practical, faithful example gives hope and help to churches everywhere.
>
> To them and to their church, *Guideposts* is proud and happy to present its 1972 Church Award.

That such accolades are not excessive is the opinion of many thousands of Christians from every denomination who have been touched deeply by Redeemer parish since 1964.

In less than eight years a large Episcopal church in Houston's changing inner city has undergone an astounding metamorphosis. The time factor alone is incredible; but a glance at official records further reveals that the circumstance could only be described as a soverign act of God.

Parish enrollment in 1963 was about nine hundred persons, of whom one-third were inactive because of their living situation in suburbs far from the declining parish neighborhood. About four hundred of the remainder were confirmed communicants. In 1971 the enrollment was fourteen hundred active persons, about half of whom were confirmed. In addi-

tion to growth there had been a fresh air of genuine ecumen-
icity breathed into Redeemer's corporate life, and with it was
worked a reversal of the pattern of inner-city abandonment—about a hundred and fifty families had moved into
Houston's East End to be close to the church. Parish reports
to the diocese show that in 1963 income from pledges and
offerings was an amount less than $40,000. The staff con-
sisted of one ordained priest and two sextons who guarded
the property at all times. Income for 1971 was $220,000
administered by a staff of four in orders and thirty full-time
lay persons; there have been no membership canvasses to
raise funds since 1967, and pledge cards are a thing of the
past. The Rector of any Episcopal parish would be surprised
and flattered were he to see an average of two-thirds of his
flock in the pews week by week. The average weekly atten-
dance at services held in 1971 at Redeemer Church was
2,200—more than 150 percent of membership.

I have called these closing remarks an interlude because so
much more needs to be told before the miracle of Redeemer
parish has been fully divulged. There is no reason for the
yarn to stop spinning in the near future, but enough of the
cloak is now in evidence to offer a confident hope to those
who love the Church and whose hearts burn to see the name
of Jesus alive in her once again.

> Awake, awake,
> put on your strength, O Zion;
> put on your beautiful garments,
>   O Jerusalem, the holy city;
> for there shall no more come into you
>   the uncircumcised and the unclean.
> Shake yourself from the dust, arise,
>   O captive Jerusalem;
> loose the bonds from your neck,
>   O captive daughter of Zion.

(Isaiah 52:1,2,3)

My life and ministry are of necessity at the heart of this
present story of threads and fabric—a fact for which I am

137

disinclined to be apologetic. In 1963 God enticed me to Houston, and in less than a year I was almost pathologically compelled to share the gospel with one of its declining East End neighborhoods. By 1965 a vision of how God would do it emerged out of my own failure, and compulsion turned into dogged determination to see it realized.

All the while we were a *bona fide* Episcopal Church.

We still are. Our relationship to the Episcopal Diocese of Texas is intimate in mutual dependence, it is cordial in shared concerns, and we enjoy warm and open fellowship. I am sure there were times during the early days when the Bishop of Texas wondered what sort of monster had been spawned by the ship channel in East Harris County Convocation. But he is a man of wisdom and patience, possessing the essential charisma of Christian leadership, which allows others to become in Christ what He calls them to be.

Upon receiving the baptism in the Holy Spirit in 1964 I became a charismatic. The signs and wonders that have attended my ministry ever since have brought many under conviction of their own impotence. To begin with several of them joined me—some to commiserate and some to support. Looking more like a gaggle of geese than a band of stalwarts, we were eventually visited by forces of dispersion that scattered all but the stout-hearted. God drew these latter together into a charismatic community whose obvious marks were intense love, indomitable faith, and a spirit of praise. In that ground was planted the seed of a renewed parish.